AMERICAN ARMOR
IN THE PACIFIC

CASEMATE | ILLUSTRATED

CASEMATE | ILLUSTRATED

AMERICAN ARMOR IN THE PACIFIC

MIKE GUARDIA

CASEMATE | ILLUSTRATED

For Marie and Melanie

CIS0012

Print Edition: ISBN 978-1-61200-8189
Digital Edition: ISBN 978-1-61200-8196

Text by Mike Guardia
Profiles by Battlefield Design
Maps by Battlefield Design
Photo retouching by Remy Spezzano
Design by Battlefield Design
Printed and bound by Megaprint, Turkey.

CASEMATE PUBLISHERS (US)
Telephone (610) 853-9131
Fax (610) 853-9146
Email: casemate@casematepublishers.com
www.casematepublishers.com

CASEMATE PUBLISHERS (UK)
Telephone (01865) 241249
Fax (01865) 794449
Email: casemate-uk@casematepublishers.co.uk
www.casematepublishers.co.uk

Title page: Two tanks from the 767th, nicknamed *Lucky Tiger* and *Miss Dinah*, return from destroying Japanese bunkers on Ebeye Island on Kwajalein, February 1944.
Contents page: An M4 with a retrofitted dozer blade moves forward during the fighting near Lantap on Luzon. The tank, belonging to the 775th Tank Battalion, was one of many Shermans in both Europe and the Pacific that carried plows or dozer blades to clear obstacles.
Map: Pacific Campaign

Note: vehicle illustrations and profiles are not to scale.

Contents

Timeline of Events

From Pearl Harbor to Okinawa, the Pacific Theater of World War II was known for its intensity and brutality. From among the island battlefronts, American and Japanese soldiers fought one another on land, at sea, and in the air. But fewer engagements were as intense—or as unsung—as the tank battles that occurred on the craggy islands of Tarawa or the forbidding jungles of Luzon. In battles large and small the American M3 Stuarts and M4 Shermans squared off against their battle-hardened Japanese adversaries.

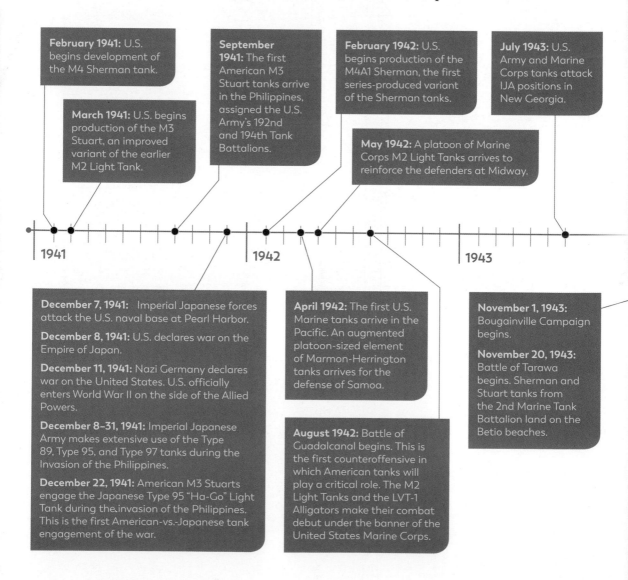

February 1941: U.S. begins development of the M4 Sherman tank.

March 1941: U.S. begins production of the M3 Stuart, an improved variant of the earlier M2 Light Tank.

September 1941: The first American M3 Stuart tanks arrive in the Philippines, assigned the U.S. Army's 192nd and 194th Tank Battalions.

February 1942: U.S. begins production of the M4A1 Sherman, the first series-produced variant of the Sherman tanks.

May 1942: A platoon of Marine Corps M2 Light Tanks arrives to reinforce the defenders at Midway.

July 1943: U.S. Army and Marine Corps tanks attack IJA positions in New Georgia.

1941   1942   1943

December 7, 1941: Imperial Japanese forces attack the U.S. naval base at Pearl Harbor.

December 8, 1941: U.S. declares war on the Empire of Japan.

December 11, 1941: Nazi Germany declares war on the United States. U.S. officially enters World War II on the side of the Allied Powers.

December 8–31, 1941: Imperial Japanese Army makes extensive use of the Type 89, Type 95, and Type 97 tanks during the Invasion of the Philippines.

December 22, 1941: American M3 Stuarts engage the Japanese Type 95 "Ha-Go" Light Tank during the invasion of the Philippines. This is the first American-vs.-Japanese tank engagement of the war.

April 1942: The first U.S. Marine tanks arrive in the Pacific. An augmented platoon-sized element of Marmon-Herrington tanks arrives for the defense of Samoa.

August 1942: Battle of Guadalcanal begins. This is the first counteroffensive in which American tanks will play a critical role. The M2 Light Tanks and the LVT-1 Alligators make their combat debut under the banner of the United States Marine Corps.

November 1, 1943: Bougainville Campaign begins.

November 20, 1943: Battle of Tarawa begins. Sherman and Stuart tanks from the 2nd Marine Tank Battalion land on the Betio beaches.

A flamethrower tank from the 713th Tank Battalion, blazes an enemy position on Okinawa, May 17, 1945.

July 21, 1944: Battle of Guam begins. U.S. Army's 706th Tank Battalion and the 3rd Marine Tank Battalion demolish the enemy's Type 95 and Type 97 tanks.

January 9, 1945: Battle of Luzon begins. U.S. Army 716th Tank Battalion engages elements of the IJA's 2nd Armored Division.

August 6 and 9, 1945: Two separate atomic bombs are dropped over Hiroshima and Nagasaki on the Japanese mainland.

1944

1945

December 1943: Elements of the Marine 1st Tank Battalion assault Cape Gloucester in the Solomon Islands.

June 15, 1944: Battle of Saipan begins. This is the first of the Mariana Islands to be conquered by American forces. The 4th Marine Tank Battalion meets elements of IJA 9th Tank Regiment in a contest of fire.

February 19, 1945: Battle of Iwo Jima begins. Marine Corps lands its 3rd, 4th, and 5th Tank Battalions against the IJA's 26th Regiment.

September 2, 1945: Empire of Japan surrenders. World War II comes to an end.

February 1944: Campaign for the Marshall Islands begins. U.S. Army's 767th Tank Battalion and the 4th Marine Tank Battalion assault positions on the Kwajalein and Eniwetok atolls.

September 15, 1944: Battle of Peleliu. In perhaps the most intense tank engagement of the Central Pacific, the 1st Marine Tank Battalion engages a company of Japanese Type 95s on the island's airfield.

April 1, 1945: Battle of Okinawa begins. Eight U.S. Army tank battalions and two Marine tank battalions land ashore for the final battle against the IJA. U.S. Army's 193rd Tank Battalion suffers heavy losses at the hands of the Japanese, but American forces still win the battle.

| Introduction

From the attack on Pearl Harbor to the nuclear devastation of Hiroshima and Nagasaki, the Pacific Theater of World War II was the most destructive conflict in human history. At the cutting edge of battle—in meat-grinder engagements like Tarawa, Iwo Jima, Saipan, and Guadalcanal—the M3 Stuart and M4 Sherman tanks fought a ferocious enemy who was prepared to fight to the death. Pitted against the battle-hardened forces of Imperial Japan, American tank crewmen nevertheless defeated the Rising Sun with a primitive fury. The Imperial Japanese Army (IJA), for its part, fielded their own tanks—namely the Type 89, Type 95, and Type 97—but none could adequately stand against the M4 Sherman in battle.

While combat in the European and North African theaters consisted of several high-profile armor engagements (Kursk, El Alamein, Hurtgen Forest, et al), the amphibious nature of

An M4 Sherman nicknamed *Lucky Legs II* from the 754th Tank Battalion leads an attack followed by soldiers of the 129th Infantry Regiment during the Bougainville Campaign. Given the terrain in the Pacific Theater, tanks performed best when operating as part of a tank-infantry team.

the Pacific Theater relegated the tank to an infantry support weapon. Indeed, because of the tropical vegetation and the islands' terrain, there were no tank-on-tank battles to the scale of what was seen on mainland Europe. Of the 70 separate tank battalions fielded by the U.S. Army during World War II, only a third of them were deployed to the Pacific. The U.S. Marine Corps, exclusively committed to the Pacific Theater, deployed all six of its tank battalions to the island battlefronts. The Imperial Japanese Army, meanwhile, deployed only its 2nd Tank Division to the Pacific. In engagements big and small, the armored forces of both sides mostly operated on terrain poorly suited for tank warfare. Nevertheless, in jungles and on beachheads across the Pacific, American tanks provided a deadly armored punch to Army and Marine Corps infantry units in battle. Against Japanese tanks, the Stuart and Sherman made short order of their mechanical adversaries. *American Armor in the Pacific* provides an illustrative look at the U.S. Army and Marine Corps tank forces in their battles against the Empire of Japan.

The Pacific War was a conflict nearly 20 years in the making. Emerging victorious from World War I, the United States and the Empire of Japan had been allies in the cause to defeat the Central Powers. However, as the post-war euphoria and the prosperity of the 1920s yielded to the economic hardships of the Great Depression, the trans-Pacific allies began to take a divergent path.

Japan was already a major power, having defeated the pride of Czar Nicholas's fleet during the Russo-Japanese War. Following the Allied victory in World War I, however, Japan began a rapid and comprehensive program of industrialization and rearmament. Indeed, while their Western allies focused on domestic recovery, Japan sought to expand its sphere of influence. These overtures for expansion began in the Chinese province of Manchuria.

Although territorially a Chinese possession, Manchuria had, in essence, been a Japanese protectorate since the end of the First Sino-Japanese War. That eight-month conflict (July 1894–April 1895) ended in a decisive victory for the Empire of Japan. It yielded significant territorial gains for the Rising Sun and precipitated the rapid downfall of the Qing dynasty. By 1930, Japan's influence in Manchuria had become undeniable: indeed, the Japanese owned the provincial railroads, had made numerous financial investments, and had a few thousand security troops garrisoned in the province (i.e. the so-called "Kwantung Army").

China, however—reasserting its sovereignty and still stung by its defeat during the Sino-Japanese War—began challenging the Japanese presence on Mainland China. Rather than honor Chinese sovereignty, however, Japan launched a full invasion of Manchuria in 1931. China appealed to the League of Nations, but when that international polity censured Japan, the Rising Sun simply withdrew from the League.

Almost simultaneously, the Japanese military underwent a radical change in its way of thinking. A reintroduction (and subsequent perversion) of the bushido warrior code had brainwashed an entire generation of Japanese soldiers into thinking that "no mercy" was the only way to conduct oneself in combat and during occupation duty. In centuries past, the *bushido* samurai stressed a humanitarian spirit and honorable behavior toward one's enemies in the wake of their defeat. By the late 1930s, however, this behavior had morphed into an inscrutable code of vicious conduct.

This newfound brutality came center stage during the Second Sino-Japanese War, in 1937. This re-initiation of hostilities brought widespread chaos and devastation to the northeastern Chinese mainland. The atrocities committed by the Imperial Japanese Army in Nanking and greater Manchuria sent shock waves throughout the civilized world. The magnitude of the death toll varies among sources, but most historians agree that between 40,000 to 300,000 Chinese civilians died at the hands of the Imperial Japanese Army. What truly shocked the international community, however, was the sheer barbarity of the Nipponese soldiers. There were mass executions, torture, rape, arson, looting, with some Japanese soldiers using live civilians for bayonet practice.

Aghast at Japan's naked aggression on the Chinese mainland, and its burgeoning alliance with Nazi Germany via the Anti-Comintern Pact (1936) and the Tripartite Pact (1940), the U.S. began leveraging sanctions against the Rising Sun. Limiting oil exports, followed by freezing Japanese assets in the U.S., these sanctions were intended to stem the tide of Japanese aggression and perhaps bring it back into the friendly fold of the World War I era.

The U.S., meanwhile, was focused primarily on the threat from Nazi Germany. By 1941, Great Britain and the Soviet Union were relying heavily on American logistics and equipment (via the Lend-Lease Program) in their struggles against the Wehrmacht. Yet, American strategic planners were convinced that the Empire of Japan posed no credible threat to the U.S. Navy. These same analysts concluded that Pearl Harbor, the Navy's principal anchorage in the Pacific, was invulnerable to any Japanese attack. Distance was the supposed ally, while the shallow depth of the harbor did not lend itself to traditional torpedo attacks.

But even if the Japanese were to initiate a naval conflict, strategists knew that the Imperial Japanese Navy could not withstand a protracted war against the American fleet. As the Chief of Naval Operations, Admiral Harold Stark, told the Japanese ambassador:

> While you may have your initial successes, due to timing and surprise, the time will come when you too will have your losses, but there will be this great difference. You will not only be unable to make up your losses but will grow weaker as time goes on, while on the other hand, we will not only make up for our losses but will grow stronger as time goes on. It is inevitable that we will crush you before we are through with you.

Still, these plausible forewarnings did not dissuade the Japanese High Command from attacking the naval base at Pearl Harbor, Hawaii, on December 7, 1941. The Imperial Japanese Navy had hoped to crush the Pacific Fleet in one blow, thus crippling America's ability to wage war in the Pacific. Ironically, the Japanese may have succeeded had the U.S. aircraft carriers not been away from Pearl Harbor on maneuver.

Nevertheless, the U.S. prepared itself for war against the Empire of Japan. As Admiral William Halsey put it: "When this war is over, the Japanese language will only be spoken in Hell."

The following day, the U.S. declared war on the Empire of Japan. With the stroke of a pen, America had officially entered World War II.

| Opposing Forces

At the outset of World War II, neither the U.S. nor the Japanese possessed a well-developed armor corps. On paper, the Imperial Japanese Army had a functioning armored force, but it was equipped with subpar tanks that were mechanically troublesome, lightly armored, and fared poorly in the field. During the war, the IJA fielded four successively numbered tank divisions. Each division came equipped with a variety of light or medium tanks.

The Evolution of Japanese Armor

Having seen the effectiveness of Allied tanks during World War I, the IJA likewise wanted to develop its own cadres for armored warfare. For field trials, the Japanese acquired several foreign tanks for evaluation. These models included a British Heavy Mark IV (purchased in October 1918), along with 13 French Renaults and six British Mark A Whippets (both of which were acquired in 1919). After successful field trials with both vehicles, the IJA officially established its armored force in 1925, making provisions for three light tank battalions and one heavy tank battalion.

However, because the Japanese had not yet developed a program for domestic tank production, the IJA solicited newer tanks from Britain and France. The wartime Allies were happy to accommodate, but the only model available was the vintage Renault FT. Reluctantly, the Japanese imported the older Renaults and, in 1927, imported a Vickers Medium C tank for study and evaluation. During field trials, however, the Vickers C's gasoline engine caught fire. This prompted Japanese designers to install diesel engines in all domestically produced tanks. By 1930, having been somewhat impressed by the early-model Renaults, the IJA acquired 10 newer Renault NC1s, which they re-designated *Otsu-Gata Sensha* ("Type B Tank"). Interestingly, the Type B was still in IJA service at the outset of World War II; and the Japanese acquired additional spare parts after occupying French Indochina. Shortly after their initial purchase of the Renault NC1, the IJA also purchased several Vickers 6-ton tanks and Carden Loyd tankettes, studying the designs for both and using them as a basis for further domestic tank production.

Not surprisingly, most of the officers, designers, and technocrats in the Japanese Army Technical Bureau insisted that future IJA tanks be made in Japan. The chief of the Technical Bureau, General Teiichi Suzuki, protested the Ministry of War's decision to purchase further British or French tanks. The Ministry eventually acquiesced to Suzuki and halted the import of European tanks in the 1920s. Almost simultaneously, a special committee of the Imperial General Staff explored the feasibility of domestic tank production and the development of tactical doctrines.

Developing the basis for tank production, however, proved to be a daunting task. For instance, the Japanese engineers had little to no experience designing, much less building,

Although not particularly well-equipped or well-developed by Western standards, the Japanese armored corps had more than 2,000 operational tanks by 1939. By the following year, the Imperial Japanese Army and the Japanese Special Naval Landing Forces—i.e. Japanese Marines—collectively had the fifth-largest tank force in the world. Most of these tanks, however, were lightly armored; the Japanese military never fully envisioned their tanks to fight as standalone weapons. To make matters worse, their tanks were mechanically troublesome and often unreliable in the field.

military vehicles. To this point, even the best engineers in Japan had only designed trucks and tractors. Compounding the problem was the Imperial government's low priority for tank steel production. Nevertheless, the Technical Bureau lumbered forward with its inaugural tank designs. Between 1931 and 1945, the Empire of Japan would produce some 6,450 tanks—more than half of which (3,300) were manufactured by Mitsubishi.

Like the Americans, the Japanese were heavily influenced by French tank designs and their attending doctrines. As with most militaries of the industrialized world, the IJA viewed the tank largely as an infantry support weapon. Indeed, the Japanese did not fully envision a role for the tank as a standalone weapon. This outlook, however, would cost the IJA terribly in battle against the Americans and the Soviets in the upcoming years.

Beginning in 1932, the Type 89 *Chi-Ro* became the first mass-produced Japanese tank. It remained the IJA's standard medium tank until the late 1930s. Although it served on the frontlines during the Second Sino-Japanese War and the Pacific Campaign, the Type 89 was nevertheless obsolete by the time it entered service. Its successor, the Type 97 *Chi-Ha*, was a marked improvement, and remained in service until 1945, but was nevertheless easy prey for Allied tanks.

During the Second Sino-Japanese War (1937–45), these early-model Japanese tanks were successful, but primarily because the Chinese had no viable armored forces of their own. The shortcomings of both the Type 89 and Type 97, however, were brought to light during the battle of Khalkhin Gol, a 1939 skirmish between the IJA and the Red Army in the Mongolian borderlands. The battle of Khalkhin Gol pitted the Japanese Type 89 and Type 97 against the vaunted Soviet BT-5 and BT-7.

During that battle, the IJA's 3rd and 4th Tank Regiments collectively consisted of:

- 8 Type 89As
- 26 Type 89Bs
- 4 Type 97s
- 35 Type 95s

Additionally, IJA infantry and cavalry units had approximately 50 to 60 tankettes and armored cars. Despite this impressive show of force, the IJA lost 42 tanks after only four days of combat. To make matters worse, the Soviets launched a counteroffensive in late August, enveloping the IJA ground forces and ensuring their destruction.

Following their defeat at the battle of Khalkhin Gol, the Imperial Japanese Army re-evaluated their tank tactics, formations, and designs. Armored production increased from

500 tanks per year to 1,200 per year. The IJA also decided that their tanks needed a stronger main gun, thus developing the 47mm Type 1 gun—subsequently mounted into the Type 97 *Chi-Ha*. The resulting up-gunned tank was re-designated the Type 97-*Kai* ("improved"), alternatively called the Type 97 *Shinhoto Chi-Ha* ("new turret"). Although still vulnerable to Allied tanks such as the M4 Sherman and Soviet T-34, the improved 47mm high-velocity gun did give the Type 97 a fighting chance against enemy tanks. By 1940, the IJA had the fifth largest tank force in the world, but was severely lacking in medium and heavy tanks—firepower that would pay the biggest dividends on the modern battlefield.

Although the IJA's tanks were soundly defeated by Red Army at the battle of Khalkhin Gol, the Japanese nevertheless continued to emphasize the tank as an infantry support weapon. With the start of the Pacific Campaign against the Americans, however, Japan shifted its priorities into the production of naval ships and aircraft. Considering the terrain of the anticipated battlespace—mostly tropical islands and rainforests—Imperial Japan did not see the need to expand its tank production any further.

In fact, throughout most of the Pacific War, the IJA's older, pre-1940 tanks saw the most action along the frontlines, normally as static defensive weapons or for direct-fire infantry support. Newer Japanese tank designs—such as the Type 1 *Chi-He* and the Type 3 *Chi-Nu*, which presumably could stand toe to toe against the M4 Sherman—did not appear until late in the war and had virtually no effect on the vitality of the IJA's frontline forces. As with many of the IJA's latter-day weapon systems, their production rarely advanced beyond the prototype stage. Moreover, due to the Allied bombing, material shortages and the loss of industrial infrastructure curtailed much of the Empire's military production.

Thus, although the IJA widely employed tanks within the Pacific Theater of World War II, it fared poorly in the face of American armor. Even as more tanks were produced, there was a strong desire within the Japanese High Command to hold them for mainland defense rather than disperse them to the far reaches of the Pacific.

Japanese Equipment

Type 94 Tankette

Perhaps the most unusual addition to the IJA's armored force was the "tankette." By definition, a tankette was a tracked, armored vehicle similar to tank, but lacking the main gun firepower and armored protection of a traditional tank. Typically, tankettes were the size of a small automobile and were used primarily for reconnaissance and infantry support. As expected, tankettes were lightly armored and their primary armament was typically a machine gun or grenade launcher.

By 1940, most militaries had abandoned the concept of the tankette, but the IJA remained one of the most prolific users of tankettes until the end of World War II. Of the few tankettes fielded by IJA, the Type 94 was its most versatile and ubiquitous. Throughout its service with the Japanese ground forces, the Type 94 served as an ammunition tractor, reconnaissance vehicle, and general infantry support although it was not intended as direct combat weapon.

An American GI inspects a Japanese Type 94 tankette after the fighting on Okinawa. The "tankette" was a brief but unusual chapter in the history of armored warfare. Conceived as a light reconnaissance and infantry support platform, the tankette was a small tracked vehicle typically armed with a machine gun as the primary armament. By the late 1930s, most militaries had abandoned the concept of the tankette, but the Imperial Japanese Army remained the most prolific user of tankettes until the end of World War II.

During the 1920s, as the IJA acquired and tested a variety of European tanks, the Japanese General Staff elected to develop a new vehicle based on the Carden Loyd Mark VI tankette design. Development of the Type 94 began in 1932, with the first prototype completed in 1934. With a lightly armored hull, the vehicle sported a front-mounted, air-cooled, gasoline engine capable of 35 horsepower. Given its size, the Type 94 could only accommodate a crew of two: a driver and vehicle commander. The armament was a singular machine gun—initially a 6.5×50mm machine gun, although later models carried a 7.7mm machine gun.

Having performed admirably in combat during the Second Sino-Japanese War, the IJA decided to retain the Type 94. By the outset of World War II, every Japanese infantry division in the Pacific had at least one company of tankettes. Throughout the war, the Type 94 tankette saw action in Burma, the East Indies, the Philippines, and several other islands in the South Pacific. They remained in service until 1945.

Type 97 *Te-Ke* Tankette

Designed as a replacement for the Type 94, the Type 97 *Te-Ke* (not to be confused with the Type 97 medium tank, discussed later in the book) was a tankette intended mostly for armored reconnaissance. Its design was similar to the Type 94, but with several modifications. For example, the new diesel engine was moved to the rear of the vehicle, while the gun turret was mounted atop the middle of the hull. And whereas the Type 94's driver had been located on the right, the Type 97's driver operated the vehicle from a left-hand station. As the IJA discovered, this configuration gave the two-man crew (driver and commander) a better means to communicate with one another.

A lesser-known Japanese tank that served during the Pacific campaigns was the Type 2 amphibious tank. Pictured here is the Type 2 *Ka-Mi*, based on the Type 95 light tank. Like its land-based counterparts, however, the Type 2 also fared poorly in combat against American armor.

Unlike its predecessor, the Type 97 tankette featured a low-caliber tank gun as its primary armament. This 37mm main gun (the same armament found aboard the Type 95 light tank) carried 96 rounds, had a muzzle velocity of 600 meters per second, and could penetrate 45mm of armor from a distance of 300 meters. However, due to the production constraints and supply shortages associated with building the 37mm gun, many Type 97 variants were equipped with a 7.7mm machine gun instead.

Like many of its stablemates, the Type 97 first saw combat against Chinese and Soviet ground forces during the latter 1930s. During the opening months of the Pacific War, the Type 97 performed admirably during the campaigns in Malaya and the Philippines. As it turned out, the Type 97's lighter weight enabled it to traverse bridges and crossings that were otherwise unsuitable for heavier tanks. The vehicle's narrow berth, meanwhile, allowed it to navigate the region's narrow roadways with ease. The Type 97 tankette remained in service through the end of the war, but had little to no effect on either American or British armor.

Type 89 *Chi-Ro (I-Go)* Medium Tank

After its abortive attempts with the experimental "Type 87," the IJA overhauled the design of that experimental tank into the Type 89 *Chi-Ro*. Weighing in at 12.8 tons, the Type 89 featured stronger and lighter steel-plate armor instead of the plodding iron armor that had been used on the Type 87. The *Chi-Ro's* main gun was a 57mm cannon, accompanied by two Type 91 6.5mm machine guns. The first prototype was completed in 1929, with full-scale production of the Type 89 beginning in 1931. Throughout its service history, the Type 89 was simultaneously called the *Chi-Ro* and *I-Go*.

A Japanese Type 89 tank, knocked out during the fighting in the Philippines. The Type 89 was one of the first tanks mass-produced for the Imperial Japanese Army. Although it performed somewhat admirably during the Second Sino-Japanese War, the Type 89 was normally the loser when pitted against American tanks.

The Type 89 had two variants: the *Ko* ("A"), with a water-cooled, gasoline engine, and the *Otsu* ("B"), which used an air-cooled, diesel engine. In total, 113 *Ko* variants and 291 *Otsu* variants were produced. Like most its early tanks, the IJA parceled out the Type 89 to its infantry divisions, wherein it first saw combat in China during the first battle of Shanghai (1932). The Type 89 also served during the Second Sino-Japanese War, where it met Soviet forces during the battle of Khalkhin Gol. However, the IJA's defeat during that battle begot the realization that the Type 89 was rapidly growing obsolete. Thus, the IJA began a program to develop a replacement tank—leading to the new Type 97 *Chi-Ha* medium tank.

Type 95 *Ha-Go* Light Tank

Almost simultaneously with the development of the Type 97 *Chi-Ha*, the Type 95 *Ha-Go* was also intended as a replacement for the Type 89 medium tank. Mitsubishi started production as early as 1936, with more than 2,000 units built by the end of the war. Despite its lighter armor, the Type 95 was highly maneuverable and had an impressive land speed among its stablemates. Armed with a 37mm main gun and two 7.7 mm machine guns (one turret-mounted, the other hull-mounted), the Type 95 weighed in at 7.4 tons and carried a crew of three.

The Type 95 served alongside the Type 89 during the battle of Khalkhin Gol, and later against the British Army in Burma and India. On December 22, 1941, the Type 95 became the first tank to engage in tank-versus-tank combat against American armor (M3 Stuarts) in the Philippines. Consequently, the Type 95 was also the only Japanese tank to have ever landed on American soil during any war, as the Philippines was still a U.S. commonwealth territory at the time.

A Japanese Type 95 light tank. Manufactured by Mitsubishi, the Type 95 was the flagship of Japanese light tanks. It served on nearly every island battle throughout the Pacific War, and was the first Japanese tank to engage American armor in combat, trading fire with M3 Stuarts during the Philippine Invasion of 1941–42.

Type 97 *Chi-Ha* Medium Tank

The Type 97 was the most widely produced Japanese medium tank of World War II. By 1930s' standards, the armor protection was adequate, but not exceptional: approximately 25mm thick on its turret sides and 30mm on the gun shield. From 1938 until 1943, Mitsubishi produced some 3,000 units, including many specialized variants. Initial versions of the Type 97 featured a low-velocity 57mm tank gun designed primarily for infantry support. After 1942, however, the IJA upgraded the Type 97 with a higher-velocity tank gun, mounted on a larger, three-man turret.

A Japanese Type 97 medium tank, the most-produced Japanese medium tank of World War II. The Type 97 saw combat throughout the Pacific War, most notably in the Philippines, as pictured here in Luzon. However, like its Type 89 stablemate, it often fell prey to American Shermans and M3 half-track field guns.

The Type 97 first saw combat during the Philippines Campaign in 1942. Although it fared somewhat poorly against Allied tanks, its high-velocity gun nevertheless gave it a fighting chance against the M3 and M4. Today, it is still considered to be the best Japanese tank to have seen combat in the Pacific Theater.

Type 98 *Ke-Ni* Light Tank

Developed in 1938, the Type 98 was designed as a replacement for the Type 95—addressing the latter's deficiencies as noted during the Second Sino-Japanese War. In the aftermath of that conflict, the IJA realized that the Type 95 was vulnerable to heavy machine-gun fire. Thus, plans were drawn for a new light tank with comparable weight to the Type 95, but with thicker armor. Although the design phase for the Type 98 began in 1938, production did not begin until 1942.

The Type 98 sported a two-man turret, featuring a 37mm tank gun, with an impressive muzzle velocity of 760 meters per second. Mounted coaxially to the main gun was a 7.7mm machine gun in a coaxial mount. Throughout its service life, a total of 104 Type 98s were built: 1 in 1941, 24 in 1942, and 79 in 1943. One notable variant of the Type 98 was the "Type 2 *Ke-To*" light tank, produced in 1944. Supposedly, the Type 2 had better performance metrics, made possible by an improved 37mm gun mounted atop an enlarged turret. However, only 34 of these Type 2s were manufactured by the end of the war, none of which engaged in combat during the Pacific Theater.

The Evolution of American Armor

In World War II, the U.S. Army ultimately fielded 16 armored divisions, along with 70 separate tank battalions, while the U.S. Marine Corps fielded six Sherman tank battalions. A third of all Army tank battalions, and all six Marine tank battalions were deployed to the Pacific Theater of Operations (PTO).

The story of American armor began in the latter days of World War I, when the U.S. joined the Allied cause in April 1917. Having watched the war progress from across the Atlantic, the U.S. was impressed by many of the technological advances that had debuted on the European battlefront—machine guns, tactical aircraft, etc. The most innovative killing machine, however, was the tank. Born independently within the British and French armies, the tank was supposedly the key to breaking the deadlock of trench warfare. The British, in particular, had been pushing the development of mobile, combined-arms strike forces with tanks leading the charge into battle. At the time, however, the U.S. had no tanks of its own. Indeed, by 1917, the U.S. Army's most mobile and rapid strike force was still the horse cavalry.

By the summer of 1917, however, after considering the French and British reports regarding tank warfare, General John J. Pershing, the American Expeditionary Force's (AEF) commander, decided that tanks would be critical to the American war effort. So began the establishment of the U.S. Army's Tank Corps.

To fulfill the needs of its wartime ranks, the U.S. Army solicited recruits for the Tank Corps by visiting college campuses and farm communities across the nation. The idea behind this recruiting strategy was to enlist (a) bright young thinkers and (b) men who had had experience operating heavy machinery in outdoor environments.

For its burgeoning Tank Corps, the U.S. Army established a single training post—Camp Colt—near the historic battlefield at Gettysburg, Pennsylvania. The camp commandant was a young Captain Dwight D. Eisenhower, who would later become the Supreme Allied Commander in Europe during World War II and served two terms as the 34th President of the United States. Because only *one* tank was available for training at Camp Colt, the Tank Corps recruits were hastily shipped to France where they were assembled into the Tank Corps School near the town of Langres. There, they trained aboard their French-built Renaults under the tutelage of Tank Corps School commandant, Lieutenant Colonel George S. Patton, Jr.

Although the United States had conducted successful tank operations toward the end of World War I, the U.S. Army had no viable armored force during the interwar years. That abruptly changed, however, following the Blitzkrieg in Europe (spearheaded by German armor) and America's officially entry into World War II following Pearl Harbor. Throughout the war, the most massed-produced U.S. tanks were the M3-series Stuart and M4-series Sherman. In total, 13,859 Stuarts were built. By 1946, 49,324 Shermans had been built.

The Tank Corps saw its first combat action during the battle of Saint-Mihiel in September 1918. Under operational command of the U.S. First Army, Patton attacked with two battalions from the 304th Tank Brigade, equipped with 144 French-built Renaults from the French. Of note is that even during his formative years as an officer, Patton had a reputation for his hard-charging, "piss-and-vinegar" approach to combat leadership. During this battle of Saint-Mihiel, and later during the Meuse-Argonne Offensive, Patton stormed through the barbed-wired, trench-laden fields *on foot* as he accompanied his tanks into battle. During the Meuse-Argonne campaign, the U.S. Tank Corps lost 27 tanks to enemy action, but lost several more due to mechanical failures and breakdowns. By the end of the war, the Tank Corps was down to less than 50 mission-capable vehicles.

Following the Allied victory, the U.S. Army quickly demobilized its wartime conscripts and underwent an intense reorganization. Although the World War I-era tanks were slow, clumsy, and mechanically unreliable, their value had been proven on the battlefields of Western Europe. Indeed, by 1919, the U.S. Army had begun categorizing tanks as "light," "medium," or "heavy"—each carrying different capabilities depending on the anticipated nature of the operational environment.

As they settled into their postwar careers, Patton and Eisenhower were committed to developing a permanent armored force within the U.S. Army. Both men envisioned using tanks in massive, standalone formations to breakthrough enemy defenses and seize territory. Unfortunately, both men met considerable opposition to their ideas from those who insisted in keeping the tank as an infantry support weapon rather than as a separate arm conducting its own operations. One of the chief proponents of this contrary view was General John J. Pershing, the former AEF commander. In fact, before a joint session of Congress, Pershing convinced the Committees on Military Affairs to keep the tank subordinate to the infantry.

Congress heeded Pershing's advice and, in passing the National Defense Act of 1920, the Tank Corps was subsumed into the Infantry.

Throughout the 1920s, military appropriations (particularly, the funding needed for tank research and development) came to virtual standstill. By 1928, however, Secretary of War Dwight F. Davis directed that a tank force be developed for the U.S. Army. Inspired by the maneuvers he had observed by the British Experimental Armoured Force, Secretary Davis was convinced that the U.S. needed to reinvest in its own armored warfare capabilities. As a result of Davis's directive, the U.S. Army established an experimental mechanized force at Camp Meade, Maryland, in the summer of 1928. Unfortunately, this experimental unit collapsed a year later due to insufficient funding. But the 1928 experiment did, however, convince the War Department of the need for a permanent mechanized force.

By 1936, the U.S. Army had committed itself to mechanizing and motorizing its formations. To this end, the Cavalry branch (still mounted on their horses) set out to develop combat vehicles that would enhance the traditional cavalry role of reconnaissance, rapid deployment, mobile firepower, and pursuit. Per the National Defense Act of 1920, however, the Cavalry was prohibited from acquiring tanks because they were tools assigned to the Infantry. Undaunted, the Cavalry simply sidestepped the law by designating their vehicles as "combat cars." In this case, the distinction between "tank" and "combat car" was largely administrative (albeit cunning) as both types of vehicles had similar designs and capabilities. For example, the resulting T7 and M1 Combat Cars were tracked vehicles that looked virtually no different than the standard light tanks of the day.

By 1940, almost fortuitously for the Cavalry branch, the ongoing war in Europe proved that armored vehicles with proper cannons, and independent formations, were needed to ensure viability on the battlefield. The T7 Combat Car was thus cancelled and the M1 was further developed into M1 Light Tank.

Finally, on July 15, 1940, the U.S. War Department created the Armored Force under the direction of General Adna Chaffee. Separate brigades at Fort Knox and Fort Benning formed the backbone of the inaugural armored divisions. From these humble beginnings, the U.S. Army's Armored Force grew to 16 armored divisions by the end of World War II. Starting with less than 1,000 World War I-era tanks in 1940, by 1945 the U.S. had produced nearly 90,000 tanks.

While the U.S. Army struggled to create a viable armored force during the interwar years, the U.S. Marine Corps took a slightly different approach to tank warfare. Like their Army brethren, the Marines, too, saw the viability of the tank. However, their lean and light structure (and their relatively low standing amongst the greater priorities of the defense budget) left the Marines with an underdeveloped tank force. During the 1920s, for example, there had been a provisional tank platoon of M1917s assigned to the Marine Corps Expeditionary Force, but it folded after only five years of operation.

During the 1930s, however, Navy and Marine Corps planners revisited integrating tanks into their joint doctrine of amphibious warfare. The Marines had recently gained a newfound appreciation for combined-arms operations during their deployments in Latin America's Banana Wars. Light tanks, they reasoned, would provide a heavy direct-fire

In Profile:
The Marmon-Herrington Combat Light Tank Series (CTLS)

Dutch Army Marmon-Herrington Tank in Surinam, 1947

The Marmon-Herrington Combat Light Tank Series (CTLS) remains one of the most curious footnotes in the history of armored warfare. Built by the automotive component manufacturer Marmon-Herrington, the namesake vehicle was a series of American light tanks initially produced for the U.S. Marine Corps, although the Marines later rejected it as a viable assault vehicle. At the start of World War II, production of the Marmon-Herrington continued for the export market. The vehicle design was unique in that it had no rotating turret, had a two-man crew, and was armed with three machine guns (two 7.62mm and one .50-caliber). Throughout the war, the few CTLS vehicles that remained in U.S. service were found mostly in Alaska, while a handful remained in the continental U.S. for coastal defense. After the war, the newly created Indonesian Army operated the CTLSs until 1949.

Although similar in size and function to the latter-day M2/M3 series tanks, the Marmom-Herrington did not have a rotating turret—thus limiting its service life.

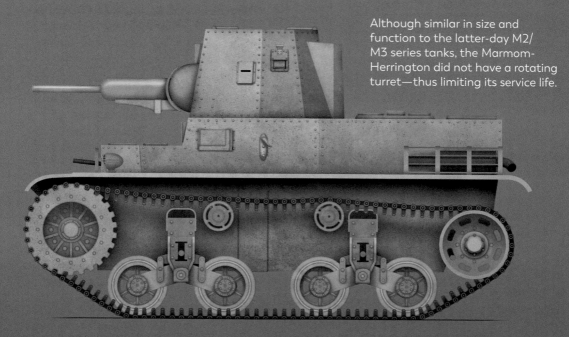

capability to seaborne infantry and augment onshore batteries, as well as offshore naval gunfire. Although suitable light tanks did not yet exist to accomplish this mission, these forward-thinking Naval and Marine Corps officers had planted the seeds for incorporating armored assets into amphibious warfare. In fact, the Marine Corps' *Tentative Manual for Landing Operations*, approved by the Chief of Naval Operations in 1934, stated:

> The primary mission of tanks in the landing operations is to facilitate the passage of infantry through the immediate beach defenses by destroying enemy wire and machine gun defenses at or near the water's edge … In addition, tanks in adequate numbers should be provided to support the advance to the final objective. Their speed and maneuverability make them particularly effective for rapid exploitation.

The manual further postulated that tanks be landed simultaneously with the infantry during the assault waves.

Shortly thereafter, the Marines established their first tank company in 1937 at Quantico, Virginia. Their inaugural tanks, however, were Marmon-Herringtons—two-man, turretless tanks with three fixed machine guns. The Marmon-Herringtons were as unreliable as they were unattractive. To make matters worse, their turretless design rendered them impractical on the modern battlefield: to aim the fixed machine guns, the driver had to turn the entire vehicle. Still, the Marmon-Herrington was light enough to meet the expeditionary needs of the Marine Corps.

Almost simultaneously, the Army and Marine Corps insisted that the U.S. Navy accommodate a greater ship-to-shore capability to meet the needs of joint amphibious operations. Specifically, the Army and Marines needed landing craft suitable for personnel and equipment. When the Navy-designed experimental boats failed to meet expectations, the Marine Corps turned to private boat builder, Andrew J. Higgins, whose eponymous "Higgins boats" became the standard amphibious landing craft for both the European and Pacific Theaters.

Meanwhile, aside from the conventional land tanks, the Marines also sought to develop an amphibious fighting vehicle. In 1937, inventor Donald Roebling appeared in a *Life* magazine article featuring his latest invention—a tracked vehicle that he called the "Swamp Gator." Serendipitously, the Marine Corps Commandant read the article, and quickly solicited Roebling and the Food Machinery Company to produce a military-grade version of the "Swamp Gator." The result was the Landing Vehicle Tracked (LVT) Alligator—a staple of Marine Corps mechanized operations throughout the war.

By the outset of Pacific Campaign, the Marines had acquired several M2- and M3-series light tanks, and already possessed a viable doctrine for integrating armored assets into the broader scheme of amphibious warfare. By this time, two Marine divisions each contained one tank battalion and an amphibious tractor (AMTRAC) battalion equipped with LVT Alligators. Furthermore, each of the division's infantry regiments contained a weapons company with a pair of M3 half-tracks, armed with a 75mm antitank gun.

An M2A4 Light Tank from the 1st Marine Tank Battalion is lowered onto a transport in preparation for the fight on Guadalcanal, November 1942. The M2-series were among the first light tanks to see action in the Pacific Campaign.

American Equipment

M2 Light Tank

The first American tank to see combat in the Pacific was the M2 Light Tank. After a somewhat tumultuous design process, the M2 entered production in 1935. The first iteration, however, featured only a .50-caliber machine gun in the turret, accompanied by a .30-caliber machine gun in the hull. Following two more iterations (M2A2 and M2A3), and reviewing operations in the Spanish Civil War, the U.S. Army decided that it needed tanks armed with direct-fire cannons instead of only machine guns. The next iteration of the M2—designated M2A4— thus carried a 37mm main gun and 1-inch (25mm) armor. Powered by a 7-cylinder gasoline engine, the M2A4 also featured improved suspension and an upgraded transmission.

Production of the M2A4 began in May 1940 at the American Car and Foundry Company, a railcar manufacturer based in St. Charles, Missouri. Production of the M2A4 continued through mid-1941, with a total production run of 375 tanks. Soon thereafter, the assembly line converted to producing the new M3 Stuart Light Tank.

Although the M2 Light Tank was neither glamorous, nor particularly reliable, the War Department nevertheless viewed it as a stop-gap measure to fill the Army's immediate tank needs until a better design could be fielded.

By December 1941, most operational M2A4s in the U.S. Army were used for training. The U.S. Marine Corps had ordered the forthcoming M3 Stuart Light Tank, but since the

The M2 Light Tank only saw combat in American service with the Marine 1st Tank Battalion on Guadalcanal. The British had ordered 100 M2A4s in 1941, of which 36 were delivered. The fate of these remains unclear but there is evidence to suggest that the British Army used the M2A4 in combat with the 7th Royal Hussars and the 2nd Royal Tank Regiment during their campaigns against the Japanese in Burma and India.

M3 had yet to enter production, the Marines received 36 M2A4s as a stop-gap for their burgeoning tank forces. Undaunted, the Marines deployed several of these tanks to the Pacific. For instance, during the battle of Guadalcanal, the M2A4s assigned to Company A, 1st Tank Battalion, were parceled out to the infantry units. In this capacity, the M2A4 provided mobile fire support to attacking Marine infantry, and were especially useful in disabling Japanese bunkers. During defensive operations, M2A4s and M3 Stuarts would operate in pairs, covering each other with interlocking machine-gun fire against Japanese assaults.

Following the Guadalcanal campaign, the Marine Corps determined that the 37mm main gun was insufficient to engage the existing fleet of Japanese armor. After the Japanese defeat at Guadalcanal, Company A, 1st Tank Battalion returned to Australia, whereupon they replaced their M2A4s with the new M4 Sherman. A few M2A4s remained in service in the Pacific Theater until 1943, when it was withdrawn from frontline service.

M3/M5 Stuart Light Tank

The M3 Stuart grew out of the U.S. Army's program to improve the M2 Light Tank. Observing German panzer operations in Europe, American tank designers realized the M2 couldn't stand toe to toe against the latest German armor. Upgrading the M2 with thicker armor,

An M3A1 Stuart tank on Guadalcanal. Before the arrival and full integration of the M4-series Sherman, the M3 Stuarts were the premier tanks of American ground forces in the Pacific.

Unlike its M2 forebear, the M3 Stuart had a long postwar service history. Although the Americans promptly abandoned the vehicle toward the end of World War II, the M3-/M5-series Stuarts served with the Chinese Nationalist Army during the Chinese Civil War during the late 1940s. In fact, under the Chinese Nationalist forces, the M5A1 would have its finest hour during the battle of Kuningtou in 1949, for which it came to be known as the "Bear of Kinmen." British M3A3s saw action during the Indonesian National Revolution, but suffered heavy losses due to its thin armor plating. They were used until 1946, when the British left. The M3A3s then remained in service with the Indonesian National Army for the next few years. South Africa continued to use M3A1s until 1968. Over the next several decades, the Stuarts remained in service with the armies of Portugal and El Salvador. Surprisingly, the M3 Stuart remains in service with the Armed Forces of Paraguay, although largely relegated to a training role.

a better suspension, and an improved gun recoil system, the Army re-designated it as the "Light Tank, M3." Mass production of the vehicle began in March 1941 and continued until late 1943.

Like its immediate predecessor, the M2A4, the M3 was initially armed with a 37mm main gun and five .30-caliber machine guns. The first machine gun was located coaxially with the main gun, the second on top of the turret, the third mounted on the right bow, with the fourth and fifth mounted respectively in the left and right hull sponsons. Later, the main gun was replaced with a slightly longer M6 variant, but it retained the 37mm caliber. Also, the sponson machine guns were eventually removed. Despite its designation as a "light tank," the Stuart was surprisingly heavy in its armor. For instance, the upper and lower front hulls respectively had 38mm and 44mm armor plating. Meanwhile, there was 51mm of armor on the gun mantlet and 38mm on the turret sides.

Most of the M3 variants built were powered by an air-cooled, 7-cylinder Continental W-670 radial gasoline engine—although nearly 1,500 Stuarts were powered by 9-cylinder Guiberson T-1020 diesel engines. Ironically, both powerplants had originally been developed as aircraft engines. For either engine aboard the M3, it was located at the rear of the tank while the transmission stood in the front of the hull. The engine's crankshaft, however, stood high off the bottom hull, contributing to the tank's high profile.

As wartime demand for radial aero-engines grew, military planners developed a new version of the M3 featuring twin Cadillac V8 automobile engines with twin Hydra-Matic transmissions. Labeled the "M5"—since the "M4" designation already belonged to the Sherman tank—this upgraded Stuart was quieter, more spacious, and its automatic transmission simplified crew training. Although several units had complained about the M3's lack of firepower, the M5 nevertheless retained the same 37mm gun. The M5 eventually replaced the M3 in production after 1942, until it was superseded by the M24 Chaffee in 1944. In total, more than 8,800 M5 variants were built.

M4 Sherman

Perhaps the most popular tank of World War II, the M4 Sherman was developed as a replacement for the M3 Stuart. Named after the famous American Civil War leader, General William T. Sherman, the M4 was first produced at the Lima Locomotive Works in Lima, Ohio. Throughout its production run, the U.S. Army developed seven successive variants of the M4 Sherman: the M4, M4A1, M4A2, M4A3, M4A4, M4A5, and M4A6. However, these designations did not necessarily represent upgrades or improvements to the base-model M4. Rather, these successive designations represented standardized variations in production (for example, engine configurations and performance metrics). In fact, many of these M4 variants were manufactured concurrently at different production facilities.

Whatever their designation or assigned variant, most Shermans ran on gasoline-powered engines. The M4 and M4A1, for example, ran on a 9-cylinder, air-cooled Wright R975 Whirlwind 9 radial engine, producing up to 400 horsepower. The M4A3 featured a liquid-cooled Ford GAA V8 while the M4A4 used the Chrysler A57 multibank engine. The M4A2 and M4A6, however, ran on diesel engines. The M4A2 carried twin GMC 6–71 in-line engines, while the M4A6 was powered by a 9-cylinder Caterpillar RD-1820.

Over the course of their production, the M4 variants almost simultaneously underwent several upgrades to their strength and performance—all without changing the tank's basic model number. These upgrades included better suspension, improved ammunition stowage, and stronger armor.

The M4-series Sherman medium tank became the mainstay of American armored forces during World War II and, in many respects, became symbolic of the war itself. The M4 Sherman underwent many upgrades and variations throughout the war, and remained in U.S. service throughout the Korean War.

In Profile:
Japanese tanks

Japanese Type 89, Type 95, and Type 97 tanks were the workhorses of the Japanese armored corps. However, after the defeat of Imperial Japan, the World War II-era tanks were scrapped. In their stead, the reconstituted Japanese Ground Self-Defense Force (JGSDF) received, ironically, American Shermans and M24 Chaffee light tanks. However, because the typical Japanese tank crewman was much smaller and thinner than his American counterpart, the JGSDF found the Shermans to be too roomy, which prompted a revitalization of Japan's armored vehicle production, leading to the development of the Type 61 tank.

This diagram depicting a Japanese Type 95 tank appeared in the September 1944 edition of the U.S. *Army's Handbook on Japanese Military Forces.*

A side-by-side comparison of the M4A2 Sherman and the Type 94 tankette. The stark difference in size, armament, and craftsmanship underscores why Japanese armor was so ill-matched against American tanks in the Pacific.

The most iconic tank of the World War II, the M4 Sherman, has also had a long postwar service life. The U.S. maintained the M4A3E8 "Easy Eight" Sherman in service throughout the Korean War, where, on the frontlines, it fought alongside the M26 Pershing and M46 Patton. The U.S. finally retired the Sherman in 1957. The Israeli Defense Forces used the Sherman throughout the 1960s and 1970s, where it performed admirably in the 1967 Six-Day War. Like many vintage U.S. tanks, the Sherman also served in several Latin American armies through the late 20th century. The last known military to operate the Sherman was the Armed Forces of Paraguay, who retired their last three Shermans in 2018.

Central to any M4 variant, however, was its main gun armament. The earliest-production Shermans carried a 75mm medium-velocity gun. Later models—namely the M4A1, M4A2, and M4A3—received a high-velocity 76mm gun mounted to a larger turret. Later into its service life, however, the M4A3 received a 105mm gun and a distinctive rounded mantlet. In fact, the Sherman's design team had made provisions for the turret to accommodate multiple calibers of main armament. Aside from the 75mm, 76mm, and 105mm cannons, the Sherman's designers had considered mounting a 3-inch heavy tank gun to the turret of the M4, but quickly discovered that it was too unwieldly for the vehicle's body.

The Sherman entered combat in 1942 during the North Africa campaign. The first frontline Shermans came equipped with the 75mm gun, squaring off against the German Panzer III and Panzer IV tanks. Although the 75mm main gun could penetrate the frontal armor of these early Wermacht tanks, the first-generation M4s performed rather poorly against the Panther and Tiger tanks. Nevertheless, in combat against the Japanese Type 89 and its stablemates, the M4 Sherman was the heavy favorite.

LVT Alligator

Conceived by inventor Donald Roebling as a civilian rescue vehicle, the so-called "Swamp Gator" was intended to operate in marshy areas inaccessible by traditional boats. As the Marine Corps continued to develop and refine their amphibious warfare doctrine, the Commandant became interested in the Swamp Gator after seeing it featured in a *Life* magazine article.

At first, Roebling was hesitant to lend his machine to military purposes, but promptly changed his mind after World War II broke out in Europe. The first militarized prototype was completed by May 1940, followed by a second prototype that the Marines evaluated in November 1940. Impressed by the evaluation results, the Bureau of Ships placed an initial contract for 100 units of the LVT-1. Using all-steel construction, the first operational LVT-1 was delivered to the fleet in July 1941.

The LVT-1 could carry 18 personnel or up to 4,500 pounds of cargo. Although originally intended as a tactical ferry between ships and the shore, the Marines nevertheless capitalized on its utility as an assault vehicle. One of Roebling's earliest LVT designs sported a gun turret. In response, the Marine Corps recommended arming the LVT with a 37mm gun and three additional machine guns. Since the vehicle was supposed to be light and nimble, the Marines recommended armor protection capable of defending against 12.7mm machine-

The American LVT-series was perhaps the most unique armored platform sent to the Pacific Theater. Based on the civilian rescue vehicle invented by Donald Roebling, the U.S. Marine Corps adopted the LVT as its first true amphibious assault vehicle. Throughout the war, the Marines improved and upgraded the LVT-series based on the operational needs of island warfare. Pictured here is the LVT(A)-4, featuring improved armaments and defensive armor.

gun fire. These combined recommendations led to development of the LVT-2 "Buffalo." An up-armored version was later introduced, the LVT(A)-1, which was fitted with a turret from the Stuart-series tank. Other upgrades included a new powertrain and suspension which improved performance on land.

Although the battle of Midway is generally regarded as the turning point of the Pacific War, the Japanese were still on the offensive until Guadalcanal. Only after Guadalcanal did the Japanese truly go on the defensive. The constant pressure on Guadalcanal had diverted Japanese resources from other theaters, contributing to a successful Allied counteroffensive in New Guinea. In June 1943, the Allies launched Operation *Cartwheel*, which ultimately neutralized Rabaul and facilitated synchronization of the Southwest Pacific campaign under General Douglas MacArthur and the Central Pacific campaign under Admiral Chester Nimitz, both of which were critical in the drive toward Japan. For American armored forces, Guadalcanal underscored the ineffectiveness of the M2 light tank and facilitated a more rapid acquisition of the M3-/M5-series Stuart and M4-series Sherman.

Production of the LVTs continued throughout the war, with a total of 18,616 units delivered. By 1945, 11 Marine Corps battalions and 23 U.S. Army battalions were equipped with some variant of the LVT. In fact, the LVT's utility and durability were so renowned that even the British and Australian armies used the vehicle in combat.

After the war, the Marine Corps kept the vehicle in service until well into the 1950s. Today, the legacy of the LVT continues with the modern LVTP-7, the Marine Corps' primary armored amphibious assault vehicle.

M3 Half-track Gun Motor Carriage

Developed from the M3 Scout Car, the M3 Gun Motor Carriage half-track was a reconnaissance vehicle turned "tank destroyer." In the military parlance of the day, a tank destroyer was an armored vehicle with enough firepower to destroy enemy tanks, but typically lacked the mobility, maneuverability, or operational flexibility of a tank itself. The half-track concept itself, however, was devised to combine the handling of a wheeled vehicle with the cross-country durability of a tracked vehicle. After a somewhat tumultuous and convoluted design process, the base-model M3 half-track was tested by the Army at Aberdeen Proving Grounds in 1941 and was accepted into service soon thereafter.

Throughout the war, the U.S. fielded more than 40,000 half-tracks of various functions and capabilities. Indeed, half-tracks served as personnel carriers, reconnaissance vehicles, self-propelled artillery, antiaircraft artillery, and tank destroyers. Perhaps the most well-known of these half-track variants was the M3 Gun Motor Carriage.

Powered by a 147-horsepower, six-cylinder engine developed by the White Motor Company, the M3 Gun Motor Carriage was armed with a French-built M1897A5 75mm gun, which fired M61 armor-piercing rounds that could penetrate up to three inches of enemy armor. The vehicle accommodated a crew of five: commander, gunner, driver, and two loaders. From 1941 until 1943, a total of 2,202 M3 Gun Motor Carriages were produced. Production ended in 1943 as more viable tank destroyers came on line. Nevertheless, the M3 Gun Motor Carriage remained in service through the end of the war. Although the U.S. eventually retired all its half-track vehicles, the M3 variants had a viable postwar service life in the Israeli Defense Forces, serving in both the Six-Day War (1967) and the Yom Kippur conflict (1973).

M3 Half-track Gun Motor Carriage (GMC). The half-track vehicle sought to combine the handling of a wheeled vehicle with the cross-country endurance of a tracked vehicle. Throughout the war, American half-tracks were adapted into several roles, one of the most popular being the GMC. Technically a "tank destroyer," the GMC carried a 75mm gun that made short work of several types of enemy tanks in both the European and Pacific Theaters.

| Defeat in the Philippines

In the fall of 1941, American forces in the Philippines fell under the jurisdiction of the United States Armed Forces Far East (USAFFE). Commanded by an Army general, USAFFE encompassed all U.S. military assets in the Philippine archipelago. This included American ground forces, the Far East Air Force, the Asiatic Fleet, and the semi-autonomous Philippine Army. For the lean American ground forces, USAFFE's only armored asset was the 1st Provisional Tank Group, consisting of the 192nd and 194th Tank Battalions, both of which were equipped with M3 Stuarts.

Both USAFFE tank battalions had begun their service lives in the Army National Guard. The 194th Tank Battalion, for example, drew three of its companies from three different states: Minnesota, Missouri, and California. On February 10, 1941, the battalion was called into federal service and began its active duty training at Fort Lewis, Washington. Throughout the summer of 1941, the 194th honed its reputation as one of the best tank battalions in the Army. On September 8, 1941, the battalion received its orders to the Philippines along with their 54 M3 Stuart tanks. The 192nd Tank Battalion was comprised of companies from Wisconsin, Ohio, Illinois, and Kentucky. Similarly equipped with M3 Stuarts, the 192nd arrived in the Philippines that November.

Almost simultaneously with the attack on Pearl Harbor, Japanese forces invaded the Philippine Islands on December 8, 1941. The premier Japanese tanks units assigned to the invasion were the 4th and 7th Tank Regiments, equipped with Type 95 *Ha-Go* light tanks. Both the 192nd and 194th Tank Battalions sallied forward to meet the enemy during the opening days of the campaign. The first tank-on-tank engagement, however, did not occur until December 22. At the time, the 192nd Tank Battalion was commanded by Major Theodore F. Wickord. Ordered to move northward to stop the advancing enemy, Wickord sent Baker Company, commanded by Captain Donald Hanes, ahead as the battalion's lead element. During Baker Company's advance, however, Hanes received orders to intercept the Japanese mechanized force approaching the town of Damortis.

Unfortunately for Baker Company, they had not been allowed to properly refuel their tanks before receiving the order to Damortis. Thus, Captain Hanes consolidated the company's fuel into one platoon of M3s. This platoon, led by Lieutenant Ben Morin, ran headlong into Damortis on the afternoon of the December 22, where his platoon encountered a section of Japanese Type 95 *Ha-Go* tanks from the IJA 4th Tank Regiment.

The ensuing firefight was the first encounter between American and Japanese tanks. From the outset, the M3 and Type 95 were comparably armed and had similar armor protection. Thus, it seemed that victory in this engagement would belong to whoever gained the initiative and achieved the element of surprise. The lead tank in Morin's platoon immediately scrambled off the road to maneuver against the Type 95s, but the ill-fated Stuart was instantly crippled by a *Ha-Go*'s 37mm main gun. As the enemy continued scoring hits on the other four Stuarts in Morin's platoon, these beleaguered M3s withdrew from the fight, only to be destroyed later by enemy aircraft. Lieutenant Morin and his crew were later captured.

Meanwhile, 194th Tank Battalion hadn't fared much better than their comrades in the 192nd. On December 8, Charlie Company stood in defensive positions around Clark Field, where the first Japanese bombs fell. Of the nine Japanese fighters shot down that day, Private Earl G. Smith of Charlie Company shot down one of them. Thus, the 194th Tank Battalion was the first California National Guard unit to see combat, as well as the first tank unit credited with an aerial kill. As part of the ongoing defensive scheme, Charlie Company was detached from the 194th Tank Battalion and sent to the South Luzon Force on December 12, 1941. The following day, Charlie Company moved to Tagaytay Ridge, attempting to apprehend spies and saboteurs who had been setting flares near USAFFE ammunition dumps at night. These constabulary interdictions continued until the week of Christmas when General Douglas MacArthur, the USAFFE commander, ordered all forces to withdraw to the Bataan Peninsula.

On Christmas Day, the South Luzon Force commander, Brigadier General Albert M. Jones, ordered Charlie Company to engage the Japanese landing force at Mauban. To that end, Jones himself decided to lead a reconnaissance of the area, borrowing a Charlie Company half-track. Jones and his reconnaissance patrol soon came under fire from a Japanese advanced guard near the town of Piis. During the firefight, Charlie Company's half-track became incapacitated and fell into a ditch, but the crew was able to carry the vehicle's machine guns back to the American patrol base.

Japanese Type 89s during the invasion of the Philippine Islands, 1941. At the outset of the invasion, the only American armored units defending the Philippines were the 192nd and 194th Tank Battalions, both of which had been federalized National Guard units. Although the American tank crews defended valiantly, they were eventually overwhelmed by the Japanese invasion force.

The following day, Charlie Company's 2nd Platoon was ordered to attack the Japanese contingent at Piis. The platoon leader, Second Lieutenant Robert F. Needham, suggested a reconnaissance of the area prior to the attack, but his superiors told him it was unnecessary—a fatal error in their judgement that would cost Needham his life. Due to the previous night's firefight with the half-track, the Japanese had prepared a roadblock consisting of antitank guns, machine guns, and artillery pieces with barrels lowered into direct-fire mode. As Needham in the lead tank advanced upon the Japanese position, the enemy opened fire, making Needham's tank the first casualty of the day. The second tank in Needham's patrol, commanded by Staff Sergeant Emil S. Morello, drove around Needham's tank and literally ran over one of the Japanese antitank guns before his own tank was disabled by enemy fire. Soon, all five tanks in the platoon had been immobilized, with five crewmen killed. The Japanese, believing that all the American crewmen had been killed, simply moved on past the tanks, continuing south toward Bataan. The oversight was fortuitous, however, as it allowed Sergeant Morello to evacuate the wounded.

By January 1, 1942, both the 192nd and 194th Tank Battalions had begun taking up positions in and around Bataan. Their first duty in that regard was guarding the bridges over the Pampanga River, leading into Bataan proper. Coincidentally, Charlie Company, 194th, was the last unit to cross the Pampanga bridges before they were demolished to slow the Japanese advance.

While covering the American retreat to Bataan, the 194th Tank Battalion saw its first tank-on-tank action. As it turned out, a group of IJA Type 89A tanks was on approach. Having not conducted a reconnaissance beforehand, these Type 89s were oblivious to the M3 Stuarts that were lying in wait. The Stuarts destroyed the Japanese tanks in short order.

Following a few more weeks of delaying actions and covering patrols, the 1st Provisional Tank Group formed its last defenses on Bataan. During the final Japanese attack on Bataan, Able Company from the 194th Tank Battalion was assigned to the coastal defenses, firing upon Japanese vessels to keep them from coming ashore. Charlie Company, meanwhile, along with the 45th Infantry Regiment, counterattacked northward on April 7. In the ensuing action, Charlie Company made contact with elements of the IJA 7th Tank Regiment, destroying two Type 89A tanks.

On April 9, the 1st Provisional Tank Group was ordered to pull all of its tank off the line. That evening, USAFFE ordered its troops to destroy their equipment and surrender. Following the surrender of American forces, several captured tank officers were interrogated by the Japanese. During questioning, the American tank crewmen learned that that their M3 Stuarts had dissuaded the Japanese from invading across Manila Bay, and that the Japanese tank crews actually feared the Stuarts.

Several troops from the 192nd and 194th, however, were forced onto the infamous Bataan Death March. Those who survived the brutal march were thrown into Japanese prison camps, where they were subjected to some of the most horrific living conditions imaginable. Others, however, evaded captured and joined various American–Philippine guerrilla units that harassed the IJA until Allied forces returned in 1945. Still, the losses to the 192nd and 194th Tank Battalions are hard to ignore. For example, of the 593 men assigned to the 192nd Tank Battalion in 1941, only 265 survived the war.

Major tank engagements of the Pacific campaign

Guadalcanal: Aug 1942—Feb 1943
Bougainville: Oct 1943—Mar 1944
Tarawa: Nov 1943 Enewetak: Feb 1944
Saipan: Jun—Jul 1944 Guam: Jul—Aug 1944
Peleliu: Sept—Nov 1944

PACIFIC OCEAN

HAWAIIAN ISLANDS

Pearl Harbor

Midway Island

US Pacific Fleet movements

LIMIT OF JAPANESE EMPIRE

TARAWA

GILBERT ISLANDS

Wake Island

ENIWETOK

BOUGAINVILLE

SOLOMON ISLANDS

Truk Island

SAIPAN

CAROLINE ISLANDS

RABAUL

IWO JIMA

MARIANA ISLANDS

GUAM

PELELIU

GUADALCANAL

NEW GUINEA

Port Moresby

Tokyo

JAPAN

OKINAWA

LUZON

Leyte Gulf

Nagasaki

Manila

CHINA

Singapore

AUSTRALIA

Japanese controlled territory

35

Determined to reconquer the Pacific, American tankers fought their first decisive engagements on Guadalcanal. Pictured here is a column of M2A4 light tanks from the 1st Marine Tank Battalion. During this campaign, Marine tankers developed a grudging respect for Japanese infantry. Because the enemy did not possess any viable antitank weapons at the time, they often charged the American tanks, jumping on the vehicles and trying to pry open the hatches with bayonets.

Southwest Pacific Campaign

Having suffered a devastating defeat at Pearl Harbor, and having lost the Philippines, and Wake Island, U.S. forces were determined to reconquer the Pacific. Despite the "Europe First" strategy, the U.S. War Department nevertheless ensured that viable, well-trained forces were sent to the Pacific Theater. Following the Allied defeats of 1941–42, the first use of American armor in the re-conquest of the Pacific occurred in the Solomon Islands. Of course, the dense jungle terrain impeded their operations, but these tanks were nonetheless effective when working in tandem with the infantry.

On August 7, 1942, Able Company from the 1st Marine Tank Battalion hit the shores of Guadalcanal. Throughout the day, the Marines conducted *five* separate landings, each of which led to a bloody fight, the intensity of which not even the Marine commanders had foreseen. As the IJA had no viable antitank weapons on Guadalcanal, they resorted to their own version of a land-based *kamikaze* charge. Indeed, IJA foot soldiers would charge the M3 Stuarts on foot, and climb aboard, hoping to fire through the vision slits, or drop a grenade down an open hatch. Though audacious, these *banzai* charges were rarely successful. Most of the IJA infantry that jumped onto the Stuarts were cut down by U.S. infantry, or the machine

A Marine M3 Stuart camouflaged under palm leaves during the battle for Guadalcanal. Although the terrain was not well-suited for tanks, their firepower and protection were indelible assets for Army and Marine Corps infantry.

An abandoned Japanese Type 97 tank on Guadalcanal.

The fight for the Solomon Islands continued on New Georgia into the summer of 1943. Here, a pair of M3A1 Stuarts from the 9th Marine Defense Platoon conduct a patrol near the Munda Airfield in August 1943.

The 2nd Marine Tank Battalion was activated on December 20, 1941, at Camp Elliott, San Diego, California. Per the standard Marine Corps organizational standards, the battalion had a headquarters, service, and four lettered companies: Able, Baker, Charlie, Dog, according to the pre-1954 phonetic alphabet. Baker Company deployed to Samoa in January 1942, while Charlie Company deployed to the Solomon Islands. The "2nd Tanks," as they were called, participated in every combat action of the 2nd Marine Division during World War II, including Tarawa, Saipan, and Okinawa. After the war, 2nd Tanks served a brief tour in Occupied Japan before returning to its permanent garrison at Marine Corps Base Camp Lejeune.

guns from other nearby tanks. As expected, this close-quarter fighting was anything but dignified. Upon seeing the blood-splashed tanks after the first day of fighting, the 1st Marine Division commander remarked that the Stuarts were "looking like meat-grinders."

Able Company was later reinforced, followed by Baker Company of the 2nd Marine Tank Battalion in November. At around the same time, the Japanese landed another task force intended for a counterattack across the Matanika River. Supporting this new task force were 12 Type 97 *Chi-Ha* tanks from the 1st Independent Tank Company. However, most of these tanks were destroyed by the Marines' 37mm antitank guns while crossing the Matanika.

Ironically, the five-month battle for Guadalcanal seemed to produce more casualties as a result of tropical disease than enemy action. Several American tankers, and their infantry comrades, fell victim to malaria and dysentery. Such was the toll from disease and enemy action that the 1st and 2nd Marine Divisions were out of action for nearly a year. Still, the Marine M3 Stuarts continued to fight in the Solomons alongside their Army brethren—often spearheading charges in places like Rendova, Munda, and Arundal.

An M3A1 provides direct fire support for Marine infantry in New Georgia during the fall of 1943.

It was around this time that Army and Marine tank crews began experimenting with flamethrower adaptations. At first, these experiments included nothing more than an infantryman standing atop the tank with a flamethrower manpack. Later, some crews tried attaching the flamethrower to the machine gun's ball mount turret. However, the limited range of these flamethrower manpacks (and the tanks' vibrations causing the flame propellant to malfunction) eventually prompted the crews to abandon the experiment and petition for specially manufactured flame tanks.

By July 1943, U.S. Army and Marine Corps forces had launched Operation *Backhander* on New Georgia, capturing the Munda airfield supported by Marine M3 Stuarts from the 9th Defense Battalion. The Japanese infantry, while defending New Georgia, made extensive use of magnetic antitank mines, which prompted American tankers to develop wooden and concrete add-on armor to prevent these charges from attaching to the tank.

The fighting soon spread to Bougainville in November 1943, one of the longest and bloodiest campaigns in the Southwest Pacific. Marine Corps M3 light tanks and Army M4 Shermans cut through the enemy defenses, operating primarily as infantry support weapons. The Marine 3rd Tank Battalion, for example, helped capture the Cape Torokina airfield but became bogged down by heavy rains and the dense vegetation. But nowhere was the terrain more unforgiving than at Cape Gloucester. Together with Australian forces, U.S. tankers landed in December 1943, but some of the enemy redoubts were so inaccessible that the Shermans had to be mounted aboard landing craft and used as impromptu battleships to blast enemy targets near the shoreline. Farther west, on Biak Island, Shermans from the U.S. Army's 603rd Separate Tank Company made short order of six Type 95s stationed there.

An M3A1 Stuart tank crew from the 3rd Marine Tank Battalion pose for a group photo during a lull in the fighting on Bougainville, October 1943.

As the campaign for the Solomon Islands continued, the Army advanced through Bougainville. Under the cover of a Sherman tank, nicknamed *Lucky Legs II*, American infantrymen from the 129th Infantry Regiment (37th Infantry Division) move forward to seize another objective.

On Bougainville, another Sherman tank, *Popeye III*, provides support to the advancing infantry. This close-quarters fighting in the dense jungle became the norm throughout the Pacific campaign, necessitating tight communication and teamwork between the tanks and the infantry.

Separate tank battalions, such as the 767th, 775th, were U.S. Army tank formations used throughout the European and Pacific Theaters. These numbered battalions were typically attached to infantry, armored, or airborne divisions according to operational needs. The tank battalions often floated from one division to another, but at least one battalion, the 745th Tank Battalion, spent the entire war attached to just one division. Originally, the Army wanted to create a mix of light tank battalions and medium tank battalions. However, the limitations of the M3/M5 Stuart during tank-on-tank battles, and the increasing number of available M4 Shermans, eventually swayed Army planners to use both light and medium tanks within the *same* battalion. The tank battalion consisted of three medium tank companies and one light tank company. Each medium tank company had 17 Shermans in three platoons of five tanks, with two tanks assigned to the company headquarters. The light tank company had 17 M3 or M5 Stuarts and was organized almost identically to the Sherman tank company, minus the assault gun. These battalions also had a service company, a headquarters company, a section of M4 or M4A3 105mm assault guns, and a mortar platoon equipped with half-tracks.

In all, the American Stuarts and Shermans performed admirably in the Southwest Pacific, but their utility was limited as the terrain was not necessarily conducive to sustained tank operations. What was clear from the battles on Guadalcanal and Bougainville was that, in the jungle environment, tanks performed best when operating as part of a tank-infantry team. This synergy created a remarkable "see-and-shoot" combination that exponentially increased the viability of American ground forces in the Pacific Theater.

By the close of 1943, having subdued most of the Japanese garrisons in the Southwest Pacific, the Allies turned their attention to the Central Pacific strongholds, where the terrain would be somewhat more favorable to tank operations.

Shermans from the 754th Tank Battalion along the Bougainville coast, March 1944.

| Central Pacific Campaign

As the Allies moved into the Central Pacific, the terrain on the islands became somewhat more conducive to tank warfare. Granted, it would never provide the maneuver space needed to replicate the tank battles in the European Theater, but the mid-Pacific islands nevertheless gave American armor a chance to shine both as an infantry-support weapon and against enemy armor. In contrast to the Southwest Pacific islands, the Central Pacific saw tanks used in larger numbers and employed in more innovative ways. Indeed, one groundbreaking innovation born of the Central Pacific campaign was the flamethrower tank.

The Japanese, meanwhile, had no viable antitank capabilities until the arrival of the Type 1 47mm antitank gun in the summer of 1944. Until then, however, the IJA had devised a number of bold and innovative antitank tactics, including magnetic mines, lunge mines, and satchel charges. Often, these antitank measures were preceded by the deployment of smoke grenades to mask the approach of the tank-killing teams. Despite this audacity and innovativeness, however, these tactics were costly in terms of personnel. Indeed, these exposed tank-killer teams were often cut down by Shermans, Stuarts, or the attendant U.S. infantry. In this regard, the key to the Americans' success lay in the tight communication and tactical cooperation of the tank-infantry team.

Tarawa

The first and perhaps most brutal engagement of the Central Pacific campaign occurred on the Tarawa atoll, one of several atolls scattered among the Gilbert Islands. Beginning on November 20, 1943, the battle for Tarawa pitted the 2nd Marine Division against the IJA's 6th Yokosuka and 7th Sasebo Special Naval Landing Forces (SNLF). The SNLF was the Japanese equivalent to the U.S. Marine Corps. Entrenched among these consolidated SNLF forces were seven Type 95 light tanks. The American tanks supporting the 2nd Marine Division's assault were the M4A2 Shermans belonging to Charlie Company of the I Marine Amphibious Corps (IMAC) Tank Battalion, and the M3A1 Stuarts from Baker Company and Charlie Company of the 2nd Tank Battalion.

Accompanying the tanks into battle were nearly 100 LVT-1 and LVT-2 Alligators. In fact, the November 20 landings on the Betio islet marked the first time that the Alligator landed under enemy fire. During the first three waves of the assault, LVT-1s and LVT-2s carried troops to the beach under limited protection. Lightly armored as they were, the LVT-2s had proven their worth as a reliable and resilient landing vehicle. The LVT-1, however, had not fared as well. In fact, these contested landings on Tarawa were the impetus for the

Betio Island, Tarawa Atoll

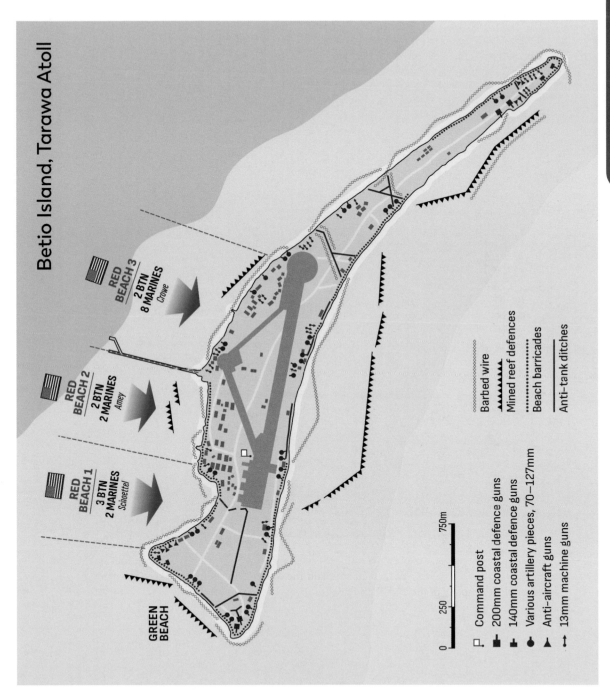

RED BEACH 3
2 BTN
8 MARINES
Crowe

RED BEACH 2
2 BTN
2 MARINES
Amey

RED BEACH 1
3 BTN
2 MARINES
Schoettel

GREEN BEACH

⌐	Command post	∿∿∿∿ Barbed wire
◼	200mm coastal defence guns	▲▲▲ Mined reef defences
◼	140mm coastal defence guns	••••••• Beach barricades
●	Various artillery pieces, 70–127mm	—— Anti-tank ditches
▲	Anti-aircraft guns	
↑	13mm machine guns	

0   250   750m

In Profile:
2nd Marine Division

Following the Allied victory on Guadalcanal, the 2nd Marine Division withdrew to New Zealand for refitting and recuperation. On July 20, 1943, the Joint Chiefs of Staff directed Admiral Nimitz to prepare for offensive operations in the Gilbert Islands. The decision to target the Tarawa atoll in the Gilbert Islands stemmed from the need to establish forward air bases capable of supporting operations in the mid-Pacific. To bridge American forces to the Philippines, the U.S. planned to seize the Mariana Islands. However, the Marianas were heavily defended, and naval doctrine held that cyclic air support was needed to cover the Allied invasion force. The nearest islands capable of supporting these combat air patrols were the Marshall Islands, which were still in enemy hands but less defended than the Marianas. Securing the Marshall Islands would provide the needed bases to launch aerial patrols over the Marianas, but the Marshalls were cut off from direct communication with Hawaii by a Japanese base on Betio islet, on the western side of the Tarawa atoll. Thus, the Americans devised their plan to seize Tarawa.

Tanks from the 2nd Marine Division fight their way through the deadly skirmishes at Saipan.

The battle for Tarawa was perhaps the most intense of the early island campaigns. Charlie Company, I Marine Amphibious Corps Tank Battalion, equipped with M4A2 Shermans, supported the initial assault. However, most of Charlie Company's tanks never made it to the beach. Of the tanks that did make it ashore, most were stymied by shell craters left by Allied naval gunfire. Pictured here is a knocked-out Charlie Company tank, nicknamed *Condor*.

The two M4A2 Sherman tanks nicknamed *China Girl* and *Colorado*, which distinguished themselves in combat during the fight for Tarawa.

The crew of this M3A1 Stuart tank, *Columbus*, poses for a photo after the battle for Tarawa. *Columbus* was one of the few tanks from Charlie Company that landed safely ashore during the amphibious assault.

An LVT-1 amtrac lies stalled upon the beaches of Tarawa. The LVT Alligator, in its various incarnations, proved to be a reliable asset in the amphibious landings throughout the Pacific. In total, 1,225 LVT-1s were built, nearly all of which served in the Pacific Theater.

development of the LVT(A)-1, the up-armored variant with a turret-mounted gun. Following the battle of Tarawa, all base-model LVT-1s were relegated to uncontested landings.

The first American tanks to hit the beach on D-Day, November 20, were six Shermans from Charlie Company, IMAC Tank Battalion. As the six fully armed Shermans waded ashore, however, one of them was disabled when it fell into a bomb crater caused by Allied naval gunfire. Having lost one of their posse, and blocked from moving forward by the piles of dead and wounded U.S. infantry, the now-five Marine tanks sallied toward the flanks of the beach, attempting to maneuver their way through the shallows of the surf. Chafingly, three more tanks flooded their engines when they, too, fell into bomb craters made by friendly fire. Now, the two surviving tanks—nicknamed *Chicago* and *China Gal*—began moving inland.

A knocked-out Sherman gives mute testimony to the brutal fighting on Tarawa.

The 2nd Marine Tank Battalion assembles its vehicles for repair and recovery on Betio toward the end of the Tarawa campaign.

A knocked-out Japanese Type 95 belonging to the 7th Sasebo Special Naval Landing Forces (the Japanese equivalent of the U.S. Marines). The Japanese employed several Type 95s for the defense of Tarawa.

While scanning the area for enemy activity, *Chicago* was knocked out, and *China Gal*'s turret ring was disabled after sustaining a lucky hit from a Type 95 Ha-Go. Undaunted, the driver of *China Gal* gunned his throttle and rammed his tank into the offending Type 95. This bold maneuver certainly rattled the enemy tank, but it simultaneously disabled the Sherman's main gun. Beating a hasty retreat, the ailing *China Gal* returned to the beachhead, where she supported the advancing infantry with her machine gun.

Meanwhile, eight Shermans from Charlie Company's 2nd and 3rd Platoons arrived on Red Beach 3. As they waded ashore, however, these tanks, too, lost one of their number to a shell hole. The three surviving tanks of 2nd Platoon advanced onto Red Beach 2. Barely a few minutes onto the beach, however, one tank was knocked out by a Japanese magnetic mine. Moments later, a second tank was immobilized by yet another shell hole.

By the following day, November 21, 2nd Platoon had recovered two of their Shermans and sent them back into the fight. The recovered firepower was short-lived, however, as

U.S. Marines inspect another Japanese Type 95 on Tarawa.

While the Marines took Tarawa, the U.S. Army's 193rd Tank Battalion landed on the nearby Makin atoll. During the fight for Makin, however, the 193rd fielded the outdated M3 Lee medium tank (not to be confused with the M3 Stuart light tank). The 193rd was the only Army unit in the Pacific to operate this tank. Here, an Army M3 Lee plows through the dense foliage on Butaritari, one of the islands in the Makin atoll.

An M3 Lee moves forward to support the 165th Infantry Regiment on Makin, November 1943.

both tanks were lost later that day: one to the seemingly endless network of bomb craters, the other accidentally disabled by a U.S. mortar team. Meanwhile, all four Shermans in 3rd Platoon were knocked out, three from enemy fire, and one from a U.S. dive-bomber in yet another case of fratricide. However, one Sherman tank from 3rd Platoon, *Colorado*, was back in action after her driver extinguished the flames by driving the tank into the surf.

Later that night, one of the disabled tanks from the initial landings on Red Beach 1, *Cecilia*, returned to the battle and spent the remainder of D+1 fighting alongside *China Gal* and *Colorado*.

For the 2nd Tank Battalion, however, none of their M3A1 Stuart tanks made it to beach on D-Day. Indeed, all four landing craft that carried Charlie Company's 2nd Platoon tanks sunk before they hit the shore. Two M3s made it into action on November 21, but one was lost to a magnetic mine. The other two platoons from Charlie Company landed all 12 of their Stuart tanks on November 22. The 18 tanks in Baker Company, meanwhile, began landing on the 21st, but lost five of their Shermans due to engine flooding and the ubiquitous bomb craters.

As the two companies rolled inland, the Stuarts' canister rounds made short work of the Japanese infantry. The 37mm gun, however, proved ineffective against the Japanese bunkers. Seeing their main guns having little to no effect on the IJA strongholds, some frustrated American tankers drove their Stuarts directly up to the bunkers and fired, point blank, into the gun slits.

Seventy-six hours after the initial landings, the Marines had secured the Betio islet. More than 1,100 Marines had been killed during the engagement with an additional 2,290 wounded. The Japanese, for their part, fared much worse, losing 2,600 troops and 2,200 civilian laborers killed.

Reviewing the outcome of the battle, however, the Marines concluded that the M3 Stuart was inadequate for sustained armored combat. The M4 Sherman, however, had certainly proven its worth as an offensive and defensive weapon. But it seemed that the greater concern was how to overcome the Japanese bunkers. Much to the Americans' surprise, these ferro-concrete bunkers had been remarkably resilient in the face of the Stuart's and Sherman's main guns. To that end, the Army and Marine Corps began to develop the flamethrower tank—designed to spit fire into the enemy bunkers.

As the Marines secured Betio, the U.S. Army's attack on neighboring Makin Island was comparatively quick and relatively painless. During the attack, the Army landed elements of the 193rd Tank Battalion, while the IJA had assigned two Type 95 light tanks to the island. However, neither of these armored assets met one another before the island was pacified.

In addition to its M3 Lees, the 193rd Tank Battalion also deployed the M3A1. A company of M3A1s fought in the Makin operation. Here, an M3A1 Stuart moves forward to interdict Japanese snipers on November 20, 1943.

In Profile:
M2 Light Tank

The M2 was the first pre-war modern tank for the U.S. Army and Marine Corps. Built by Rock Island Arsenal, the tank saw limited service in the opening days of the Pacific Campaign. Almost simultaneously, the M2 was also used by the British Army. The most-produced variant of the M2 was the M2A4, numbering 375 units in total. The M2 series was later developed into the M3/M5 Stuart, which saw more extensive use during the Pacific and North Africa campaigns.

An M2 Light Tank, 1st Tank Battalion, U.S. Marine Corps, 1942. Its only combat action was in Guadalcanal.

A crewman from Charlie Company, 193rd Tank Battalion, attempts to attach a tow cable to his immobilized M3A1 Stuart. Throughout the Pacific, several American tanks fell victim to antitank ditches, or shell craters made by naval gunfire.

Marshall Islands

As the U.S. military secured the Gilbert Islands, they cast their eyes toward the Marshall Islands, the next step in their island-hopping campaign to Tokyo. The Marshall Islands had been a German colony since their purchase in 1899 until the end of World War I. Following the Treaty of Versailles, the Marshall Islands were among a handful of German territories in the Pacific that were ceded to Japan. As part of the so-called "Eastern Mandates," Japan had kept the Marshalls relatively isolated from the outside world.

After losing the Solomon Islands and New Guinea, the Japanese High Command decided that the Marshall Islands were "expendable" and began to reinforce the IJA's defenses closer to the mainland. Nevertheless, the Marshalls were heavily fortified and were sure to present a challenge for the Allied invaders.

For American tank units, the biggest combat action occurred on the atolls of Kwajalein and Eniwetok. The Kwajalein atoll was defended by elements of the Japanese 1st Amphibious Brigade and the 2nd Mobile Battalion—numbering about 5,000 troops in total. Expecting a bloodbath similar to what had occurred on Tarawa, the Americans committed a larger landing force to the Kwajalein atoll: the U.S. Army's 7th Infantry Division and the 4th Marine Division would form the nucleus of the assault force. Supporting them were the 4th Marine Tank Battalion and the Army's 767th Tank Battalion.

A knocked-out tank from the 4th Marine Tank Battalion on Namur in the Marshall Islands, February 1944.

During the campaign to retake the Marshall Islands, the 4th Marine Tank Battalion landed on the Kwajalein atoll. Pictured here is an M5A1 Stuart from Able Company during the fighting on Namur.

M4A2 crewmen from the 4th Marine Tank Battalion show off their latest capture, a Japanese 94 tankette, after fighting in the Marshall Islands, March 1944.

On February 1, 1944, the U.S. Army and Marines began their assault on Kwajalein. The 4th Marine Division focused its attack on the adjoining Roi–Namur Islands, while the Army units stormed the other islands within the atoll. The 4th Amphibious Tractor Battalion spearheaded the Marines' initial assault onto Roi with 75 amtracs—mostly LVT-2s with add-on armor. These initial landings at Roi were slow, laborious, and a bit clumsy due to the inexperience of the newly installed LVT crews. Luckily, the Roi defenses had been softened up by Allied naval gunfire, thus allowing these fresh Marine crews to gain a

Elements of the 767th Tank Battalion during a lull in the fight for the Marshall Islands, February 1944.

M3A1 Stuarts from the 767th Tank Battalion pause during mop-up operations on Kwajalein, February 1944.

foothold on the beach. With Marine ground forces now ashore, 10 M4 Shermans and three M5A1 Stuarts respectively from Charlie Company and Able Company, both from the 4th Marine Tank Battalion, waded ashore. In support of the advancing infantry, the two tank companies blasted their way inland, capturing the airfield in the center of the island. Within two hours, the island of Roi had fallen.

Meanwhile, on Namur, the 24th Marine Regiment was supported by 10 M5A1 Stuarts from Baker Company, 4th Marine Tank Battalion. By all accounts, the battle for Namur was the hardest fight of the day. Moments after wading ashore, however, some of the Stuarts were immobilized by the silt and the sand, but even the Stuarts that retained their mobility were swarmed by *banzai*-charging Japanese infantry. Indeed, these Namur defenders were so fanatical that were the charging the tanks at point-blank range, even climbing onto the decks and turrets. Surprised by these seemingly-suicidal enemy stampedes, the tank crewmen quickly flung the Japanese soldiers off the Stuarts using machine-gun fire and canister rounds. As these beleaguered Stuarts lumbered forward, the M4 Shermans from Roi crossed a sand spit to reinforce their comrades in Baker Company. However, by this point in the battle, the Shermans had expended so much fuel and ammunition that they had to consolidate their remaining stores into only *four* tanks—nicknamed *Jenny Lee*, *Jezebel*, *Joker*, and *Juarez*. Later that night, the four Shermans plowed through a ferocious Japanese counterattack, before leading the final assault against the IJA the following day. On Namur, the only enemy armor encountered by the Americans were a few Type 94 tankettes and a Type 2 *Ka-Mi* amphibious tank.

Meanwhile on February 1, the 7th Infantry Division attacked the Japanese headquarters on Kwajalein and other enemy positions along the surrounding islets. For the Army's portion of the assault, the soldiers employed their own 708th Tractor Battalion (Provisional), a concept they had adapted from their Marine Corps brethren. On paper, the 708th was an amphibious tank battalion, but it had not as yet received enough LVT(A)-1s to fill its ranks. Thus, operationally, the 708th became an amtrac battalion equipped with mostly LVT-2s fitted with 37mm gun turrets.

For the initial landing, the Army task force had 17 LVT(A)-1s alongside a handful of LVT(A)-2s retrofitted with manpack flamethrowers mounted to the front of the vehicles. The 708th Amphibious Tractor Battalion landed its LVT(A)-2s in the center of Kwajalein, flanked on either side by LVT(A)-1s. The unarmed LVT-2s followed in the second wave.

Accompanying the 7th Division's main body were the vehicles of the 767th Tank Battalion, including M4A1 Shermans, M5A1 Stuarts, a platoon of M10 Tank Destroyers and flamethrower tanks. In total, there were 72 tanks dispersed among the 10 different islets that the Americans had to seize. After barely a week of fighting, the Kwajalein atoll fell to the Americans— due in no small part to the effectiveness of American tanks and amtracs.

Another M3A1 Stuart from the 767th Tank Battalion supports the 7th Infantry Division during its advance on Carlson Island on the Kwajalein atoll.

In Profile:
M4 Sherman

The M4-series Sherman was the most produced and most popular American tank of World War II. Throughout its service life, there were several variants of the M4 Sherman, though most variants were produced during overlapping time periods, not successively to one another. Upgrades included high-caliber main guns and stronger armor. During the war, several Shermans were given to the British and Soviet Armies as part of the Lend Lease Program. During the Pacific Campaign, Shermans were frequently the victors against the qualitatively inferior Japanese tanks.

This M4 Sherman (Composite Hull), nicknamed "Lucky Legs II" by her crew, belonged to the 745th Tank Battalion. This tank led an attack with soldiers of the 129th Infantry Regiment during the Bougainville Campaign in the fall of 1943."

The relatively swift victory on Kwajalein allowed Admiral Nimitz to accelerate operations in the Marshalls, invading Ebeye Island, Engebi Island, Eniwetok Island, and Parry Island all by the end of February 1944. The fight for Kwajalein also showed the Japanese that their beachline defenses were too vulnerable to naval gunfire. In the campaign for the Mariana Islands and beyond, the Japanese restructured their defenses in depth, using tanks both as frontline interdictors and in-depth gun positions. The defenses on Guam and Peleliu, for example, were much harder to overcome.

On the neighboring atoll of Eniwetok, the American assault followed a similar pattern. Just as they had done on Kwajalein, U.S. naval forces initiated offshore gunfire to disrupt the Japanese coastal defenses. Almost simultaneously, LVT-equipped amphibious tractor units set the initial beachhead, followed quickly by Sherman and Stuart tank landings. For the Eniwetok assault, the Army's 708th Amphibious Tractor Battalion launched its LVT Alligators, while both the Marine's 2nd Separate Tank Company and the Army's 766th Tank Battalion provided the Shermans' armored punch.

Starting on the morning of February 18, 1944, Sherman tanks blasted away at the IJA defenders on Engebi Island. Meanwhile, the light tanks of Charlie Company, 766th Tank Battalion, supported the 106th Infantry Regiment in its fierce fight on Eniwetok proper. Having made minimal progress against the stubborn defenders on Eniwetok, the Shermans from Engebi came over to assist. During the course of the ensuing firefight, American forces overran a handful of Type 95 *Ha-Go* light tanks.

By the morning of February 22, it was clear that the Americans had seized the advantage. The enemy's frontline beach defenses had collapsed and the M4 Shermans were making short order of the Type 95s. Despite losing both ground and numbers to the advancing Shermans and Stuarts, the enemy tank company held fast until the last of its Type 95s were destroyed on Parry Island. During the following weeks, the Allies captured and secured 29 other islets along the Eniwetok atoll.

A side-by-side comparison of the M4A2 Sherman and the Type 94 tankette. The stark difference in size, armament, and craftsmanship underscores why Japanese armor was so ill-matched against American tanks in the Pacific.

A Sherman from the Marine 2nd Separate Tank Company moves forward during the fight on Eniwetok in the Marshall Islands, February 1944.

Another Sherman from the 2nd Separate Tank Company supports the infantry during the fight for the Marshall Islands. Note that the Sherman is equipped with its "snorkel" fording apparatuses. These modifications enabled the Shermans to operate in the shallow lagoons and low-level flood plains of the Pacific Islands.

Mariana Islands

After pacifying the Marshall Islands, the Allies cast their attention toward the Mariana Islands, the first of Japan's so-called "inner defensive belt" that would be fiercely defended by the IJA. Indeed, the Marianas and other islands within the inner belt had airfields capable of deploying aircraft within striking distance of the Japanese mainland.

With this defensive posture in mind, the Japanese had steadily reinforced their garrisons in the Mariana Islands, augmenting the defenders with the IJA's 9th Tank Regiment. On paper, the 9th Tank Regiment was the best mechanized outfit available to defend the Marianas, equipped with the Type 95 *Ha-Go* tank, the Type 97 medium tank, and the newer Type 97 *Shinoto Chi-Ha* tank, this latter which could presumably face off against the M4 Sherman. The regiment's 1st and 2nd Companies were stationed on Guam, while the 3rd, 4th, and 6th Companies were deployed to Saipan. Meanwhile, the IJA's 24th Independent Tank Company (equipped with Type 95s) had likewise been sent to Guam, while nine Type 95s of an SNLF company joined the defenders on Saipan. Adding to their collective firepower was the new Type 1 47mm antitank gun.

At 0700 on June 15, 1944, the U.S. Army and Marine Corps began their assault on Saipan. That morning, amtracs from both services carried elements of the 2nd and 4th Marine Divisions to the beach in a two-pronged attack. Part of this amphibious assault force included the now-reconstituted 708th Amphibious Tank Battalion, having been upgraded from its previous "tractor" designation. In the days following the assault on the Marshall Islands, the 708th was the first unit of its kind to see combat with a full inventory of tanks. The battalion consisted of a headquarters company equipped with three LVT(A)-2s and

A Marine M3A1 Stuart from the 3rd Marine Tank Battalion prepares for action, 1944.

An M4A2 Sherman from the 4th Marine Tank Battalion is lowered onto a landing craft in preparation for the battle on Saipan, June 1944.

An M5A1 Stuart and its crew from Dog Company, 762nd Tank Battalion, pose for the camera following the invasion of Saipan. Although the Stuart was obsolete compared to German armor, the M3/M5 performed admirably against the lighter and clumsier tanks of the Imperial Japanese Army.

Tank crewman from the 4th Marine Tank Battalion pose with their "Satan" flamethrower tank on Saipan. The "Satan" was little more than a modified M3 Stuart and had limited success on the Pacific battlefront. Nevertheless, these flamethrower variants were helpful flushing out Japanese bunkers during the more intense battles of the Pacific Theater.

A knocked-out Type 97 (foreground) and a Type 95 (behind), both from the Japanese 9th Tank Regiment, provide mute evidence of the horrific battle on Saipan. Of the 44 Japanese tanks that fought in Saipan, only 12 survived. Looking closely at the Type 97 in the foreground, one can see numerous piercings from American armor rounds.

Another disabled Type 97 from the 9th Tank Regiment on Saipan. This tank, belonging to the regiment's 5th Company, was likely the victim of an M5 Stuart from the 762nd Tank Battalion.

LVT(A)-4s, the latter carrying a higher-caliber, open-topped turret. Two of the battalion's companies supported the 4th Marine Division landings on the southern beach of Saipan. As the Americans hit the beach, they sustained heavy losses from enemy mortar and artillery fire. Heavy as these losses were, the 708th still managed to secure a beachhead and received the Presidential Unit Citation for its role in the battle.

Later during the afternoon of June 15, the 2nd and 4th Marine Tank Battalions waded ashore on Saipan. At the start of the invasion, however, both battalions had been refitted with M4A2 Shermans, having dispensed with their erstwhile light tanks. For the operation, both tank battalions had an additional complement of M3A1 "Satan" flamethrower tanks—designed to make short order of the Japanese bunkers, or any stalwart tank-killer teams.

Once on the beach, the Marine Corps Shermans began pounding away at the enemy gun emplacements. The Japanese, aware that they were losing the fight for the beachhead, called upon an SNLF detachment supported by Type 2 amphibious tanks (highly modified Type 95s with special buoyancy apparatuses). The Marines, however, alerted by the noise of what seemed to be an approaching mechanized force, called for the offshore naval guns to fire illumination shells over their position. The astute call paid off, for as soon as the Marines saw the advancing Type 2s under the sudden illumination, they cut into the enemy tanks with a fusillade of bazooka and Sherman main gun fire.

The following day, Marine Shermans broke out from the beachhead, followed by the LVT(A)-1 and LVT(A)-4 Alligators. The LVT(A)-4 was a welcome asset on the island battlefront, carrying an improved armored punch with its higher-caliber gun. Moving

A Marine Sherman, nicknamed *Jenny Lee*, on Saipan near Magicienne Bay, July 1944. This tank carries wood planking on its side. As the Japanese had grown adept at using magnetic antitank mines, American tank crews resorted to plating their tanks with wood panels to negate the magnetic attraction.

A knocked-out Type 95 light tank from 4th Company, 9th Tank Regiment, near Black Beach 3 on Saipan.

inland, the tank commanded by Sergeant Robert McCard became isolated and immobilized by Japanese artillery. McCard ordered his crew to evacuate while he continued to hold the enemy at bay with the tank's machine gun and a few hand grenades. However, the Japanese overwhelmed the tank, and the young sergeant was killed. McCard was posthumously awarded the Congressional Medal of Honor, one of only two tankers from the Pacific Theater to receive the award.

A specially modified M3A1 "Satan" flamethrower tank escorts an LVT-series Alligator during the fighting on Saipan, July 1944. As the Americans continued their "island hopping" campaign in the Pacific, they fielded more flame-throwing tanks as a countermeasure to the ferro-concrete Japanese bunkers.

Shortly thereafter, the U.S. Army's 27th Infantry Division came ashore, supported by elements of the 762nd and 766th Tank Battalions. Representing the 762nd were Baker Company (Shermans) and Charlie Company (Stuarts), while the 766th sent its own Dog Company (also equipped with Stuarts) into the fight.

Under pressure from the American advance, Japanese commanders ordered a desperate counterattack. Selected to lead the counteroffensive was Colonel Hideki Goto, commanding officer of the IJA's 9th Tank Regiment. From the outset, however, Goto realized that the odds were stacked against him. Of the 90 tanks initially assigned to his unit, 44 had been detached to Guam, while 11 had been lost during the opening volleys on Saipan. Nevertheless, he assembled what remained of his unit and advanced to meet the American invaders. However, the noise of the force was detected by two Marine battalions, which in turn called up a platoon of Shermans from Able Company, 2nd Marine Tank Battalion, along with several M3 half-tracks.

At 0300 on June 17, 1944, the IJA's 9th Tank Regiment spearheaded the largest armored attack of the island campaign. But their audacious maneuver would not be successful. Exposed by U.S. naval illumination rounds, the lead tanks were quickly destroyed by American bazooka teams and 37mm gunfire. Amidst the chaos of battle, other Japanese tanks wandered into a swamp, where they became immobilized, and subsequently became "turkey shoot" targets for American antitank fire.

An M4A2 Sherman from Charlie Company, 4th Marine Tank Battalion, provides covering and suppressive fire for Marines near Marpi Point on Saipan, July 1944.

Another M4A2 Sherman, nicknamed *Jungle Jim*, negotiates an obstacle on Saipan, July 1944.

At daybreak, the M3 half-tracks, along with the Shermans, continued firing on the knocked-out Japanese tanks—lest they somehow be salvaged by the enemy. Of the 35 Japanese tanks that had begun the assault, by midday only 12 survived: six Type 97s and six Type 95s. Of these survivors, six were later destroyed by the Shermans from Charlie Company, 2nd Marine Tank Battalion, while the other six fell to Army M5A1 Stuarts. All the while, the newly fielded flamethrower tanks cleared enemy bunkers and caves with commendable results.

Through the battle for Saipan, both Army and Marine tankers marveled at the suitable terrain. For many of the tank crews, Saipan had been the most "tank-friendly" terrain they had yet encountered in the Pacific. Despite the ease in maneuverability, however, tank crew losses were still relatively high. The biggest culprits were artillery and magnetic mines. Similar to what had occurred on Tarawa and in the Marshall Islands, the Japanese were growing increasingly bolder in their personnel-launched antitank measures. Saipan was finally secured on July 9, 1944.

The next major tank engagements in the Marianas occurred on the islands of Tinian and Guam. The fight for Tinian began on July 24, 1944, with a landing force from the 4th Marine Division, supported by the 2nd and 4th Marine Tank Battalions. The IJA was defending the island with its 18th Infantry Regiment, accompanied by 12 Type 95 *Ha-Go* tanks. Similar to what Colonel Goto had done on Saipan, the Japanese commander on Tinian sacrificed most of his armored assets during a counterattack on the first night of the invasion. The U.S. amphibious force commander had anticipated that the Japanese would try to frontload their tanks, and thus modified the Marine landing force accordingly. Indeed, the Marines ensured that they landed sufficient armor and artillery before nightfall, and reinforced the perimeter defense with tanks and artillery from the 2nd Marine Division.

Unlike Saipan, the Japanese counterattack was well planned and deliberate in its execution. However, despite the enemy's careful planning and battlefield performance, the IJA was no match for the combined-arms presence of American tanks, infantry, artillery, and naval gunfire. Simply put: the IJA was outgunned and outnumbered. Coming off the beach, the Marine tanks crews encountered only light resistance, destroying two Type 95s in the process. As night descended over the island, the Marine tanks moved farther inland where they encountered more Type 95s arrayed in a night counterattack formation. But like their comrades on Saipan, they were also cut down. By daybreak on July 25, five additional Type 95s had fallen to American fire.

For the next week, the Marines enjoyed a form of combat rarely seen at this stage in the Pacific War: a frightened enemy on the run, desperately trying to flee the onslaught on American armor. Within nine days, Tinian fell to the Americans, at the loss of only 326 killed.

Meanwhile, Army and Marine Corps elements stormed the beaches on Guam. Whereas Tinian had been relatively easy, Guam was more costly and required a higher concentration of forces. The 3rd Marine Division and the Army's 77th Infantry Division formed the nucleus of the assault force. Accompanying these main bodies into battle were the 1st Provisional Marine Brigade, the 2nd and 4th Marine Tank Companies, and the Army's 706th Tank Battalion. Defending the island were the 1st and 2nd Companies of the IJA 9th Tank Regiment, the beleaguered tank force that had already seen many of its personnel and equipment destroyed on Saipan. Still, on Guam, the 9th Tank Regiment boasted 29 fully functioning Type 97s and Type 95s. Meanwhile, the 24th Independent Tank Company had nine Type 95s.

M3A1 Stuarts flanked by a "Satan" flamethrower during the fighting on Saipan. Flame tanks were typically accompanied by conventional tanks for bunker-busting missions.

A platoon of Shermans from Charlie Company, 706th Tank Battalion, during operations in Guam, August 1944.

This Marine Corps Sherman, nicknamed *Toro*, from the 2nd Separate Tank Company, was knocked out during the fighting on Guam. July 26, 1944.

Crew maintenance during a lull in the fighting on Guam.

A tank belonging to Charlie Company, 2nd Marine Tank Battalion, comes ashore on Tinian, July 1944.

On Guam, however, the Japanese commanders deployed their tanks in piecemeal fashion, rather than committing them all in a massive counterattack: the Type 95s and Type 97s operated within small hunter-killer teams, usually at night, while maximizing their use of jungle foliage for cover and concealment. As expected, the Shermans prevailed in the tank-on-tank battles, but one Sherman was catastrophically destroyed by a 1,000-pound bomb that had been converted into an improved explosive device.

On the first day of the land battle—July 21, 1944—the Japanese destroyed 20 LVT Alligators offshore, but the tide quickly turned in favor of the Americans as they hit the beach. Five Japanese Type 95s attacked the beachhead that morning, all of which were promptly destroyed by American bazooka teams and M4 Shermans from the Marines' 4th Separate Tank Company. The remainder of the IJA 9th Tank Regiment's 1st Company was destroyed by the 2nd Separate Tank Company, while three more enemy tanks were destroyed from the air. Throughout the day, the IJA 24th Independent Tank Company was systematically wiped out with its futile counterattacks.

At this point, the remaining Japanese tanks withdrew northward to Tarague, and began their series of night attacks, supported by infantry. Five Type 97s survived a nighttime assault on August 8/9, largely because the Marines' bazooka charges had been rendered ineffective by the incessant rain. The following day, Shermans charged the last enemy stronghold, destroying two tanks and discovering that the remaining tanks had been cannibalized due to a lack of fuel and parts.

For the IJA, the battles for Guam and Saipan saw the most intense tank combat of the Pacific Theater. Although the Japanese fought aggressively, and even desperately, the island

Another Sherman from Charlie Company, nicknamed *Caesar*, moves forward along the hilly terrain of Tinian. During the campaign for the Marshall Islands, U.S. armored forces outnumbered the Japanese tanks by a ratio of four to one.

Another flamethrower tank, *Ding Dong*, from the 2nd Marine Tank Battalion lands on Saipan. July 25, 1944.

battles had proven the obsolescence of the Type 95 and Type 97 in combat. Even the much-anticipated, newer-model Type 97 *Chi-Ha* tanks had proved no match for the Shermans. Making matters worse for the Japanese was that all their tanks were easily penetrated by bazooka and heavy machine-gun fire.

The fighting on Guam, Tarawa, and Saipan demonstrated that the American tank crews had solved most of the problems associated with island warfare. High-caliber armaments and flamethrowers had increased their direct-fire capabilities, and the ever-evolving "tank-infantry teamwork" had mitigated most of the IJA's aggressive antitank tactics. Still, even at this stage in the Pacific War, Allied landing craft were vulnerable to Japanese artillery.

At the conclusion of the battles on Tarawa and Saipan, General Douglas MacArthur, commander of the Southwest Pacific Area (SWPA), diverted a large number of landing craft to the invasion of the Philippines. Understandably, this left the Marine Corps and other Army elements with fewer landing assets to conduct simultaneous operations elsewhere in the Central and Western Pacific. Nevertheless, experiments had been underway to improve the fording and flotation kits for the Shermans, Stuarts, and the other armored vehicles operating in the Pacific. Reflecting on these last three island battles—Guam, Tarawa, and Saipan—the Marines discovered that although their LVTs could never substitute for tanks in combat, the amtracs were nevertheless instrumental in providing direct-fire support and offering some means of protection to infantrymen as they approached the beach.

This Sherman, *Goldbrick Jr.*, from the 4th Marine Tank Battalion, engages the enemy near the southern end of Tinian.

Peleliu

Operation *Stalemate*, the campaign to seize the island of Peleliu was, in many respects, a "meat-grinder" battle reminiscent of Tarawa. Although the fighting on Peleliu didn't reflect an internalization of the lessons learned in the Marianas, it nonetheless ended in an Allied victory. Intended as a quick, diversionary blitz to cover General MacArthur's left flank as he sailed to the Philippines, the battle for Peleliu became somewhat of a sideshow, dragging on for 10 weeks and costing nearly 10,000 casualties for the 1st Marine Division and the Army's 81st Infantry Division. To make matters worse, the victory on Peleliu yielded virtually no strategic benefit to the overall Pacific Theater.

Misplaced optimism aside, however, the American tank crews performed valiantly and aggressively along the craggy fields of Peleliu. Their performance was even more remarkable considering their logistical handicaps. To this point, the Marines had made effective use of turning their landing craft into "gunboats" by placing their tanks atop stacks of dunnage, thereby enabling the Shermans to fire over the tops of the landing craft and engage the enemy's onshore batteries. For the invasion of Peleliu, however, most of the landing craft had been diverted to retake the Philippines, thus forcing the Marines to leave one-third of their Shermans behind. Marine commanders knew that going into battle at two-thirds' strength would be costly, but they had no say in the matter. While trying to optimize their assault force to compensate for the missing firepower, Marine commanders also had to contend with delays in equipment delivery. Indeed, the 1st Marine Division's new LVT(A)-4s did not arrive until the eve of the fight. Thus, Lieutenant Colonel Kimber H. Boyer, commanding officer of the 3rd Amphibious Tractor Battalion, used factory blueprints to train his LVT crews on their battle drills and maintenance tasks.

The battle of Peleliu has often been referred to as the most difficult fight that American troops encountered during the war. In fact, the 1st Marine Division was so bloodied that it remained out of action until the battle of Okinawa in April 1945. In sum, the 1st Marine Division suffered more than 6,500 casualties on Peleliu, roughly one-third of the entire division. The U.S. Army's 81st Infantry Division also suffered heavy losses: more than 3,000 casualties during their time on the island. It is estimated that Americans troops expended more than 13 million rounds of .30-caliber ammunition, 118,262 hand grenades, and nearly 150,000 mortar rounds.

Defending Peleliu was an increasingly desperate and thoroughly agitated IJA task force, consisting of the 2nd Infantry Regiment, reinforced by two additional battalions. The main body of this reinforced regiment had 15 Type 95 *Ha-Go* tanks ready for action. Several of its troops were veterans of the Manchurian border conflict with the Red Army, and thus had more combat experience than most of the IJA soldiers the Americans had fought thus far. Their fighting skills, coupled with the unforgiving terrain, made Peleliu a formidable target. Unfortunately for the American tank crewmen, the offshore naval gunfire—which had performed so brilliantly during the fight at Guam—accomplished next to nothing on Peleliu. Indeed, during the three-day preparatory bombardment, U.S. naval gunfire had left much of the IJA's assets untouched. Even when the U.S. underwater demolition teams blew channels through the enemy minefields, the Japanese commander simply sent his best swimmers to re-sow the mines. In their haste, however, these IJA swimmers failed to properly arm the mines, thus rendering them ineffective against American tanks. Had it not been for this negligence, D-Day on Peleliu would have been much more costly.

The 1st Marine Division landed on Peleliu on September 15, 1944. As the Marines closed in on the beach, the Japanese commander decided to hold most of his forces in the highlands, hoping to goad the Americans into a battle of attrition. He did, however, send one infantry battalion and a tank company to meet the Americans on the beach. That morning, with the fourth wave of the assault, the Marine 1st Tank Battalion sent its tanks ashore. All of them were hit by Japanese gunfire. Luckily, the reinforced bow armor and "rounded obliquity" of the tanks saved all but three Shermans from being lost. Later that afternoon, the Japanese tank company, with its Type 95 *Ha-Go*s, launched a desperate attack across the island's open airfield, hoping to throw the Americans back into the sea. Given the firepower of the Marine Shermans, however, this mechanized *banzai* charge was nothing less than suicidal.

During this "Hail Mary" charge against the Shermans, the Type 95 *Ha-Go*s had empty 55-gallon oil drums latched onto their sides and rear ends, each drum containing coiled-up Japanese infantrymen. Although a highly unusual way to transport infantrymen into

A convoy of Shermans from Baker Company, 763rd Tank Battalion on Anguar in the Palau Islands, September 1944.

M4A2 Shermans from the Marine 1st Tank Battalion at the airfield on Peleliu, September 1944.

battle, it showed that the Japanese had no qualms about making unorthodox improvisations. The drawback to this method, however, was that it literally tethered the infantrymen to the tank. Thus, when the tank exploded, so did the barrel-bound infantrymen. This Type 95 attack quickly disintegrated under a fusillade of fire from American bazookas, M4 Shermans, M3 half-tracks, and naval gunfire. At first the Marine tank gunners were shocked to see that their armor-piercing (AP) rounds seemingly had no effect on the advancing *Ha-Go* tanks. However, they quickly realized that these AP rounds were simply slicing through the Type 95s like butter, penetrating one side and exiting the other. With only kinetic damage to the tank bodies, many of the Japanese drivers continued to press home the attack. Undaunted, the American gunners simply switched to high-explosive (HE) rounds and watched with

The highly decorated 1st Tank Battalion was activated on November 1, 1941 at Camp Lejeune, and was subsequently attached to the 1st Marine Division. Prior to this, however, the battalion had not existed as a whole, being activated essentially one company at a time. For instance, Able Company, activated on August 1, 1940, was initially called the "3rd Tank Company." Headquarters and Service Company along with Baker Company, and the remaining companies were activated in early 1942. Following the Japanese surrender, the battalion redeployed to North China for occupation duty in Tientsin. The "1st Tanks" stayed in this posture until January 1947, when the battalion (minus Baker Company) was relieved of its occupation duty in China and ordered to Guam. Four months later, the rest of the battalion (minus Able Company) arrived at Camp Pendleton, California on May 1, 1947, where it remained for the next three years. 1st Tanks currently resides at Twentynine Palms, California.

Peleliu, while costly, was among the most controversial news stories on the home front, due to the island's apparent lack of any strategic value. Indeed, the operation had produced more casualties than any other amphibious operation of the war, and the airfield captured on Peleliu never played a key role in any subsequent operations.

satisfaction as the Type 95s exploded into balls of fire and molten armor.

Throughout the battle, the 1st Tank Battalion had used a modest number of flamethrower tanks as their "bunker busters" of choice. However, the most effective flame-throwing apparatus was the U.S. Navy's Mark I flamethrower—which had the longest range and greatest lethality of any flamethrower then available to U.S. forces. Developed for, and mounted atop, the LVT Alligator amtracs, the Mark I had an effective range of 100 yards. Although the LVT-mounted Mark Is proved effective against the IJA's static defenses, the Marine crewmen still noted the vehicle's vulnerability. Any future flame-throwing vehicle would need to have armor protection comparable to a medium tank. Years later, these observations found their way into the development of the M67 Flamethrower Tank (a modified version of the M48 Patton tank) that served on the frontlines in Vietnam.

LVT Alligators from the 1st Amphibian Tractor Battalion on Peleliu, September 1944. At left is the LVT(A)-1, and beside it is the newer LVT(A)-4. These turret-armed LVTs numbered in the thousands and served exclusively in the Pacific Theater.

An M5A1 Stuart from the 44th Tank Battalion moves forward on Leyte Island in the Philippines, October 1944. The heaviest armored combat of the Pacific Theater—for both the Americans and the Japanese—took place in the Philippine Islands.

Western Pacific Campaign

By the fall of 1944, it was clear that the Japanese forces were on the verge of collapse. The successful Allied landings on Tinian, Guam, Tarawa, and Saipan had placed the Army Air Forces within striking distance of the Japanese mainland. Moreover, Japan's naval defeat in the Philippine Sea had effectively destroyed what remained of the Empire's carrier fleet.

The Philippines

General Douglas MacArthur's forces in the Southwest Pacific Area (SWPA) had been leapfrogging up from New Guinea in a series of smaller landings, closing in on the Philippines' southern isles. The Japanese, for their part, wagered that the Allies would try to retake the Philippine Islands and use the archipelago as a staging base for the impending assault on the Japanese homeland. Adding to the Philippines' strategic value was its proximity to the major shipping lanes carrying raw materials to Japan from Malaya and the Dutch East Indies. When planning and reorganizing their defense scheme for the Philippine Islands, the Japanese realized that the main island of Luzon would be the priority target. The Americans' recent victories in the Central Pacific, however, prompted the IJA to re-evaluate its defensive tank doctrines. Indeed, to this point, the "waterline defense" theme of the IJA's tank tactics had been a grotesque failure. On Saipan, for example, the 9th Tank Regiment had been decimated in its "Hail Mary" counterattack against the Marines. Likewise, the ill-fated company of Type 95s on Peleliu had been completely destroyed by American Shermans. Taking these lessons to heart, the IJA decided to bring the Philippine defenders farther inland, out of range from naval gunfire, and layered their defenses along a network of fortified lines, using the rugged terrain for cover and concealment wherever possible.

In mid-October 1944, U.S. forces began landing on the smaller Philippine islands in the Leyte Gulf. These initial landings had a diversionary effect on the IJA's command and staff—for they stripped Luzon of several combat divisions and sent them to reinforce Leyte. It was a costly move, however, as the IJA lost five combat divisions in the fight for Leyte. Thus, the IJA had just rendered Luzon vulnerable to the pending Allied invasion.

Seeing these developments from his perch in Luzon, General Tomiyuki Yamashita, commander of the Japanese occupation force—the IJA 14th Area Army—withdrew his forces into the mountainous Cordillera Central of Luzon. He reasoned that the Americans would eventually overrun the Philippines; but his goal was to inflict the maximum number of casualties and make the U.S. re-conquest as difficult as possible. In fact, a revised combat manual issued to the IJA's 2nd Armored Division in the Philippines stated that the ensuing battle:

> will end either in the annihilation of the American devils of in the complete destruction of our forces … Emphasis must be placed on antitank combat, especially against their heavy tanks. Our lack of armament is more than equaled by our divine ability and superior tactics.

Overconfidence notwithstanding, the biggest problem facing these Japanese defenders was Yamashita's own dismissive attitude toward the tank. Although he had employed his tank regiments with great success during the Malaya Campaign in 1941–42, he was reluctant to fully integrate the tanks into the broader defensive scheme on Luzon. As one senior Japanese officer recalled:

A pair of Japanese Type 89 tanks knocked out during the fighting on Leyte. October 23, 1944.

While supporting the U.S. Army's 96th Infantry Division, this Sherman from Baker Company, 763rd Tank Battalion, became immobilized in the soft mud on Leyte on November 23, 1944.

> Gen Yamashita, being an old-time infantry officer, did not believe in mechanized warfare. When the 2nd Armored Division landed in Manila, Gen Yamashita expressed great displeasure and was unenthusiastic about that unit from the outset. There were no tank specialists attached to Gen Yamashita's headquarters.

Another Army Sherman moves through the town of Jualita as the Allies retake the Philippines.

> So after the division landed, it was split up. The division commander's pleas to keep it together were not backed by anybody in the headquarters. Yamashita thought that if the division was split up, it could attack U.S. troops wherever they landed on Luzon. One unit could immediately engage them and could be reinforced by the division's other units. If it was concentrated in one area, Yamashita was afraid it would be annihilated by air attacks. The dispersed units served as a counterweight against U.S. airborne landings. The continual shifting of the units from place to place wore down the equipment and troops, and their consumption of rations and fuel convinced the general that they were more trouble than they were worth.

Come what may, the regiments of the IJA's 2nd Armored Division would nevertheless provide heavy fire support to the entrenched defenders on Luzon.

Meanwhile, U.S. Army Intelligence was aware of the 2nd Armored Division's presence on Luzon, but was unsure what the enemy's tactical disposition would be. Historical data suggested that the Japanese would use their armor in a decentralized fashion—supporting infantry as pell-mell direct-fire assets. But given the size and comparative firepower of the 2nd Armored Division, American planners chose to err on the side of caution; they devised an invasion plan forecasting a more synchronized and elaborate use of enemy armor. With these assumptions in mind, each of the participating U.S. corps was assigned a separate U.S. Army tank battalion for the initial landings. The U.S. Army I Corps received the inexperienced 716th Tank Battalion, while the XIV Corps paired up with the 754th Tank Battalion.

As an additional counter to the IJA's 2nd Armored Division, the U.S. Army also assigned its 13th Armored Group to the invasion force. The so-called "armored group" is one of the lesser-known formations from World War II. Devised in 1942, the armored groups were intended as tactical headquarters for the independently numbered tank battalions not assigned to a division. However, as the war progressed in both major theaters, it became clear that the infantry divisions needed tank support without being hamstrung by a separate

This Sherman, *Southern Cross*, belonging to the 44th Tank Battalion, leads a tactical column near Limon on November 28, 1944.

After storming Leyte, American forces landed on Luzon, the main island of the Philippine archipelago. Here, a Sherman from the 754th Tank Battalion rolls past the Philippine Assembly capitol building in Manila on January 9, 1945.

tactical command headquarters. Thus, the separate tank battalions, like the 716th, 754th, et al, were parceled out to the infantry divisions rather than staying consolidated under the armored groups. These armored groups continued to exist, but only as administrative headquarters and purveyors of technical support. In the case of the Philippine Invasion, the 13th Armored Group's assets—including the 44th Tank Battalion, the 775th Tank Battalion, and the 632nd Tank Destroyer Battalion—were farmed out to the U.S. Sixth Army. As the invasion force lumbered toward the Philippine Islands, the Army tank crews prepared themselves for what would be the largest, sustained tank operations of the Pacific War.

On January 9, 1945, the untested 716th Tank Battalion hit the beaches of Luzon in support of the 43rd Infantry Division. Upon landing, each of the battalion's tank companies was parceled out to the 43rd Division's organic regiments. Throughout the first week of the battle, the U.S. Army tanks operated within the standard tank-infantry roles that had become

The U.S. Army's 18th Armored Group comes ashore at Lingayen Gulf on January 11, 1945. American tanks, just as they had done elsewhere in the Pacific, were instrumental to the fighting in the Philippines. Shermans and Stuarts provided deadly fire support to the infantry and halted numerous enemy tanks.

common throughout the Pacific. During the opening skirmishes in the Cabaruan Hills on January 19, the 716th Tank Battalion's commander, Lieutenant Colonel Lorwyn Peterson, was killed in action while rescuing a fellow crewman. He was posthumously awarded the Silver Star. All told, losing their battalion commander during the second week of battle was an intense shock for the green and untested 716th. As the rest of the 716th plodded its way inland, the battalion's Charlie Company was held in reserve until January 17, when it was assigned to fight at Binalonan.

Meanwhile, on the Japanese side, the IJA's 23rd Infantry Division began its counterattack against the American invasion. Providing the armored support for this operation was the IJA's 7th Tank Regiment. On January 10, Lieutenant General Fukutaro Nishiyama, commanding officer of the IJA's 23rd Division, ordered his forces to move down into Binalonan and Urdanetta to engage American tanks operating in the Cabaruan Hills. To this end, the 7th Tank Regiment moved toward Urdanetta to attack the forward elements of the 716th Tank Battalion.

On January 14, the 23rd Division ordered four units—literally designated "Suicide Penetration Units"—to conduct a simultaneous counterattack on the American beachhead. These so-called Suicide Penetration Units contained elements drawn from three infantry regiments and the attendant Shigemi Group. The Shigemi Group—so named for its commander, Major General Isao Shigemi—was a mechanized task force containing elements of the 7th Tank Regiment, 2nd Mobile Infantry Regiment, 2nd Mobile Artillery Regiment, and a combat engineer company. Despite this impressive line-up, however, the attack on the American beachhead quickly devolved into a comedy of errors for the Japanese. Leading this initial charge against the Americans was 4th Company, 7th Tank Regiment, commanded by 1st Lieutenant Yoshitaka Takaki, supported by an infantry company detached from the 2nd Mobile Infantry. This small tank-infantry strike force was intended to launch from Manaog.

Black Beauty, a Sherman from Baker Company, 716th Tank Battalion, shortly after landing at Lingayen Gulf, January 1945.

In Profile:
LVT-1 and M3 Half-track GMC

The LVT-series and the M3 half-track series were among the most unique armored vehicles fielded by American forces. The half-track vehicle sought to combine the handling of a wheeled vehicle with the cross-country endurance of a tracked vehicle. The LVTs, on the other hand, were based on the civilian rescue vehicle invented by Donald Roebling. The U.S. Marine Corps subsequently adopted the LVT as its first true amphibious assault vehicle. Throughout the war, the Marines improved and upgraded the LVTs based on the operational needs of island warfare.

This LVT features two Browning machine guns and is powered by a 146-horsepower, six-cylinder engine. Throughout its service life, the LVT variants were nicknamed Alligators and also referred to as amphibious tractors or amtracs for short.

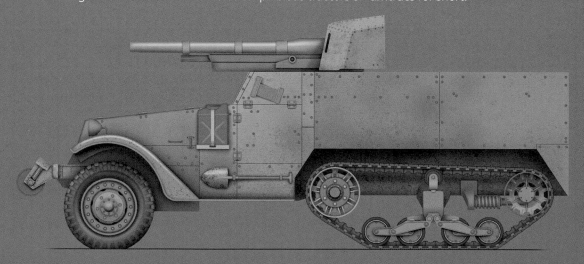

This variant of the American M3 half-track, known as the Gun Motor Carriage (GMC) was one of the most popular half-track variants of the European and Pacific theaters. Technically a "tank destroyer," the GMC carried a 75mm gun and was used extensively by both the Army and Marine Corps.

Two Japanese Type 97s, knocked out near Clark Field in the Philippines by the U.S. Army's 637th Tank Destroyer Battalion.

On the night of January 15/16, however, Takaki's patrols ran into elements of the U.S. 103rd Regiment, 43rd Infantry Division—thus making it clear that Manaog had already been seized by the Americans.

Looking for a bypass, Takaki's troops and tanks launched an attack on the village of Potpot shortly before midnight on January 17. This bold attack put Takaki's troops face to face with the 3rd Battalion, 103rd Infantry. Although the Japanese may have had the element of surprise, they quickly lost the initiative when they ran into the M4A3 Shermans that had

The lead tank of a destroyed Japanese convoy near Umungan. This lead tank was one of eight destroyed in the convoy on January 30, 1945.

91

During the fight for Luzon, the Japanese 101st Special Naval Landing Forces attempted a raid near Ormoc Bay on January 6, 1945. Among the raid's many casualties included this Type 2 amphibious tank.

just arrived from Charlie Company, 716th Tank Battalion. Following a clumsy, two-hour firefight in the dark, the Takaki-led tanks and troops quite literally hobbled out of the fray. Indeed, the Japanese lost three Type 97s, one Type 95, four other tanks disabled, and 50 troops killed.

According to one Japanese soldier's diary: "It's pitiful. The raid failed … two tank platoon commanders, and one infantry platoon leader were all killed. Six tanks were destroyed and the two infantry companies lost half their troops."

A rare Type 2 *Ka-Mi* amphibious tank, seen here after the fighting near Ormoc Bay.

Battle Baby, a tank from Baker Company, 775th Tank Battalion, negotiates a sharp curve along the Villa Verde Trail on Luzon, guided by the company commander, Lieutenant Jack Belts.

After daybreak on January 17, the 161st Infantry relieved the 103rd and continued the attack into Binalonan proper. Therein, the wounded remnants of Takaki's ill-fated raiding force had fallen in alongside the 3rd and 5th Tank Companies in a series of hasty defensive positions. At 1730 that evening, a lone Type 97 emerged from Binalonan and began firing at the American infantry. It was quickly destroyed; five more tanks emerged from the twilight before they, too, were cut down by American fire. Supported by the tanks from Charlie Company, 716th Tank Battalion, the 161st cleared Binalonan in a matter of hours. For the IJA, the 7th Tank Regiment lost nine tanks and nearly 250 troops—two of which were company commanders. Shaken, the Japanese defenders retreated to San Manuel under the cover of darkness.

Dog Company, 706th Tank Battalion, leads the U.S. 40th Infantry Division onto Negros Island in the Philippines, March 1945.

In Profile:
Pacific Adaptations

As expected, amphibious warfare brought its own set of challenges that required adaptations to ensure the viability of American armor. Therefore, a frequent sight among American tanks in the Pacific was the adaptation of a snorkel kit. These snorkels would allow the tank to wade through shallower waters without seizing the engine. Tanks could be adapted with one or two snorkels depending on the anticipated depths and/or the unit commander's discretion.

An authentic M4 Sherman tank with a snorkel kit from 1943 on display at the Welland Steam Rally in the UK, 2011. (Convery Flowers, Alamy Stock Photo)

Farther south, Able Company from the 716th Tank Battalion was attached to 3rd Battalion, 1st Infantry Regiment for the latter's attack on Urdanetta. Defending Urdanetta, however, were platoons from 3rd Company, 7th Tank Regiment, augmented by a separate infantry company. At the outset of the battle, a platoon of M4A3 Shermans led by Lieutenant Robert Courtwright tried to engage the Japanese tanks, but had trouble firing to their left flank due to friendly infantry being in their way. However, as the Shermans tried to align themselves for a clear shot, a platoon of Type 97s lay hidden in a nearby mango grove. The enemy platoon leader, Warrant Officer Kojura Wada, ordered his tanks to wait until the Shermans drew closer and to aim for the vulnerable side armor. Thus, at a range of nearly 35 yards, Wada's Type 97s opened fire on the American tanks—dismantling two Shermans, including Courtwright's tank, and blowing the track off a third, commanded by Sergeant Shrift. Despite losing its track, however, Shrift's driver was able to swing the vehicle in the direction of the offending Type 97, thereby placing the thickest armor of the tank toward the enemy. The crew of this intrepid third tank then began firing on the Type 97s, and Wada's was the first to be knocked out, sustaining direct hits to the turret and hull. The remaining tanks continued to fire on the Shermans, expending as many as 60 rounds. The second Type 97 in Wada's platoon received a direct hit from Shrift's tank. With two Type 97s now out of action, the lone surviving Japanese tank charged the Shermans in what was surely a suicidal *banzai* attack. The audacious Type 97 crew scored one ineffective hit before being destroyed by the Sherman it was trying to charge. By the end of the engagement, Able Company's total losses were one tank destroyed, two tanks disabled, two tank crewmen killed, and two wounded. Wada's platoon, however, lost all three of its Type 97s.

A Sherman tank from the 1st Cavalry Division fires on a concealed Japanese antitank gun that has moments earlier disabled another Sherman. Visible on the tank's back deck is a white star, painted upon several U.S. tanks in the Philippines to prevent fratricide from Allied aircraft.

Classy Peg, a Sherman from Charlie Company, 716th Tank Battalion, passes a knocked-out Type 97 after a battle near Linmangsen. During that battle, the 716th had supported the 43rd Infantry Division against the Japanese 2nd Armored Division.

Able Company and the rest of 3rd Battalion, 1st Infantry continued their attack into Urdanetta. The town eventually fell, with Japanese losses totaling nine tanks and nearly 100 troops. Japanese total tank losses in the U.S. I Corps sector during January 16/17 were 19 Type 97s and three Type 95s.

A rare, and intact, specimen of a Type 1 75mm self-propelled gun. Built atop a Type 97 chassis, this self-propelled mount was the only Japanese vehicle capable of destroying a Sherman at stand-off distances. However, less than a handful of these Type 1s were in service by 1945.

As the Americans pressed farther inland, the next objective was the town of San Manuel. Stung by their initial losses, the Shigemi Group was determined to halt the Americans here. This was reflected in General Shigemi's order of January 20: "The group will defend its present position to the death. The enemy must be annihilated and we will hold San Manuel at all costs." The disposition of Japanese forces in and around San Manuel also reflected this sentiment. Indeed, they had dug their tanks in to a series of revetments around the town, at hull-top defilade, with fields of fire covering all the major roads into town. Each of the more than 70 revetments was camouflaged and many were reinforced with machine-gun emplacements. Aside from these perimeter defenses, General Shigemi kept a mobile reserve force near the center of the town. This mechanized reserve was, in essence, a quick-reaction force that could support any part of the perimeter upon first contact. Although it seemed counter-intuitive to keep the IJA tanks as semi-static defenses, thus limiting their maneuverability, one high-ranking Japanese officer justified the decision:

> The employment of the tank division in the Philippines is generally considered a great blunder. The fact remains that the Americans had command of the air, preventing movement along the highways and cross-country movement in an area covered with rice paddies was impossible. Consequently, even though the tanks were organized for maneuver combat, they were immobilized because of lack of air cover and the destructive American air attacks which the tanks could not counter. They were, therefore, converted into armored, fixed defenses to be used by the infantry in key positions along defense lines. This adaptation of the tanks was so successful that, in one instance, a line 60 kilometers long was held for a period of one month.

In reality, however, none the Japanese defenses lasted more than a few days. But the officer was correct in his assessment of American air power and its effect on the IJA's mobility. More

A tactical bulldozer from the 117th Engineer Battalion recovers a Sherman immobilized by a landmine near Baguio, March 1945.

A tank from Baker Company, 775th Tank Battalion, engages a Japanese bunker along Highway 3 between Baguio and Banangan, April 1945.

to the point, it was the Americans' rapid breakout from the beachhead that eliminated the possibility of using the 2nd Armored Division as a mobile defense force. The tremendous beatings inflicted upon the Japanese armor at Binalonan and Urdanetta simply reinforced Yamashita's notion to dig his forces into the landscape, and inflict as many casualties as possible.

The U.S. Army's 161st Infantry Regiment received the task of capturing San Manuel. Commanded by Colonel James Dalton, the 161st Infantry's raiding force consisted of two rifle battalions (the regiment's organic 1st and 2nd Battalions); Charlie Company from the 716th Tank Battalion; one platoon of M5A1 Stuart tanks from Dog Company, 716th; a mortar battalion, and several rotating artillery battalions.

An M4 Sherman tank moves to occupy a hill overlooking Baguio during the attendant battle on April 27, 1945.

On January 19, Dog Company, 716th Tank Battalion, sent its platoon of M5A1s, led by Lieutenant John Griffin, on a patrol to reconnoiter the Japanese defenses around San Manuel. Supported by a section of M4A3 Shermans from Charlie Company, Griffin's platoon came under intense fire as it reached the outskirts of town. Two M5A1s were destroyed, with seven crewmen killed and one wounded. The remaining Stuarts withdrew under covering fire from the M4 Shermans.

Almost simultaneously, U.S. infantry patrols supported by Filipino guerillas began probing the defenses at San Manuel. During these probes, Colonel Dalton discovered that the northern side of San Manuel was the weakest point in the perimeter. Along this northern flank stood a ridge about 850 feet tall, which offered a superb vantage point. American patrols quickly, and rather quietly, overwhelmed the Japanese outposts along the northern flank, thereby allowing 2nd Battalion to begin its preparation for the final assault. Colonel Dalton's plan was to attack San Manuel with 2nd Battalion from the north, and 1st Battalion along the Binalonan Road. 1st Battalion would be supported by Charlie Company, 716th Tank Battalion.

At 0700 on January 24, the U.S. 25th Infantry Division launched a 15-minute preparatory artillery strike on the southwestern corner of San Manuel. As one Japanese tank crewman recalled in his diary:

> Around dawn, we received the order for all personnel to take their battle positions. I immediately jumped into the tank. The enemy artillery shelling became terrific. When the artillery finally ceased firing, I could distinctly notice the enemy automatic rifle fire sounding like roasting beans, and the sound of our heavy

The crew of *Dragon Lady*, Charlie Company, 754th Tank Battalion, poses in front of their tank during a tactical photo op in Luzon.

American soldiers in the Philippines pose in front of an M7 Howitzer Motor Carriage (HMC). Although not as ubiquitous as the Sherman or the Stuart, the HMC proved deadly in combat against the Japanese 2nd Armored Division in Luzon.

machine guns could be heard intermingled with the enemy's. Can the sound of the automatic cannon fire be the sign of the approach of the M4 tanks? At this moment, our 10cm [antitank] gun began banging away. For about an hour, its noise mingled with small-arms fire and my confidence was great. Two M4 tanks had been destroyed and one was on fire.

The M4A3 tanks of Charlie Company led the charge into San Manuel. The 25th Infantry Division's artillery barrage lifted as the Shermans passed within 300 yards of the southwestern edge of the town. Waiting silently at their defenses, the Japanese did not open fire until the M4A3s were almost at point-blank range—which, for tanks, was a distance of around 150 yards. Suddenly, the incoming Shermans were engulfed by antitank and machine-gun fire. Every available enemy weapon on the southern perimeter, including tank main guns, a 47mm antitank gun, and two 105mm howitzers were now engaging the American tanks. Several Shermans were hit, and the advance was abruptly halted by a combination of antitank fire and a nearby drainage ditch. One M4A3 attempted to jump the ditch, but became immobilized on the opposite bank. The other Shermans began firing on the Japanese positions, knocking out at least two enemy tanks.

During these opening volleys at San Manuel, the Japanese tankers performed better than even they had anticipated. One such hero of the day was Corporal Mizoguchi, commanding a Type 95 *Ha-Go*. According to Japanese records, Mizoguchi scored 18 hits against the American Shermans. The Japanese also credited one Type 97 with knocking out five M4A3s. Whatever the comparative losses may have been, the initial attack in San Manuel faltered after nearly an hour of fighting. American losses totaled one M4A3 destroyed, four disabled by enemy fire, and the one overzealous M4A3 still stuck in the ditch. Factoring in their casualties from the previous weeks, these losses at San Manuel had reduced Charlie Company, 716th Tank Battalion, to little more than half strength.

Conclusively, Colonel Dalton had not been prudent in the use of his tanks, especially in view of the M5A1 Stuarts that had been lost to enemy fire several days earlier. Like most rifle regiments, the 161st had limited experience with tanks and they had underestimated the Japanese antitank capabilities. In fact, many expected that the Sherman would be impervious to the Japanese antitank guns. While the older 37mm gun posed no threat to the M4, the new Type 1 47mm gun was a different story. The Type 1 could—and in this engagement, did—wreak havoc on the frontline Shermans. In retrospect, these Shermans could have rendered fire support to the infantry at standoff ranges, while the foot soldiers cleared the outskirts of town. Once the perimeter of antitank guns was cleared, the Shermans could have joined alongside the infantry as they cleared the town block by block.

The following day, January 25, Charlie Company, 716th Tank Battalion linked up with 2nd Battalion on the northern side of the town. Their plan was to assign an infantry scout to each tank, escorting the tank commander forward and guiding him on to the intended target. The tank commander would then direct his Sherman into an adequate position to destroy the enemy tank or antitank gun emplacement. Using this technique, the Americans cleared most of the northern half of town by January 27. To ensure the enemy's destruction, the 161st Infantry launched a two-battalion attack with Sherman tanks, eliminating several Type 97s in the process. With the Japanese defenses collapsing, General Shigemi ordered one final counterattack shortly after midnight. The 161st Infantry's after-action report described the attack as follows:

With the enemy on the run, tank crews from Baker Company, 44th Tank Battalion, pose for a cameraman on Luzon in August 1945.

The 775th Tank Battalion during a tactical pause near Baguio.

About 0100 28 January the Japs, after a great deal of preliminary maneuvering, launched an attack with thirteen tanks. The point was well selected: a salient made by the left company of the right flank battalion [1st Battalion, 161st Infantry]. Normal barrages of artillery and mortar were called in but did not quiet the Japs. The [enemy] tanks assaulted in waves of three, each tank followed closely by foot troops. The tank assault position was about 100–150 yards from our foremost elements. Riflemen in pits opposed them with rifle AT [antitank] grenades, bazookas, and caliber .50 machine guns. Two 37mm guns had the tanks within

An M4 Sherman displays the newly devised "mine flail," a curious adaptation intended to detonate antitank mines away from the hull. To this point, tank crews had already used plows and dozer blades for this purpose. The mine flail was never used in combat, and tank units had serious doubts as to whether the device would work as advertised.

range. The first tank was hit but overran the forward position, spraying blindly with machine guns and firing 47mm point-blank. Two AT guns set about 30 to 40 yards in the rear of the front elements fired on the waves in turn. Ten of the [enemy] tanks were halted, the leading one just 50 yards inside our front. All had been hit several times. Hits and penetrations were made with AT shells, AT grenades, bazookas and caliber .50 machine guns. Three tanks left the assault position and withdrew eastward out of town without attacking.

Following the failed operation at San Manuel, General Shigemi committed suicide. The 400 surviving Japanese troops, and seven surviving tanks, hobbled out of San Manuel and fled southeast toward St. Nicolas, where they regrouped with the IJA's 10th Reconnaissance Regiment. Of the 400 Japanese troops that fled San Manuel, nearly half of them were walking wounded—meaning that they were critically wounded, and likely combat-ineffective, but still ambulatory. San Manuel was declared secure on January 29, 1945. It had been a devastating loss for the Japanese: 755 killed, 41 Type 97 tanks destroyed, and four Type 95 tanks lost. The Americans, by contrast, lost only three Shermans and one M7 self-propelled howitzer.

The battle at San Manuel was the beginning of the end for the IJA's mechanized defenders in Luzon. During the first week of February, the IJA's Ida Group (with 48 Type 97s, four Type 95s, and 1,800 troops) was surrounded and destroyed near the town of Munoz.

This M4A2 Sherman is modified with an M17 multiple-launch rocket system. American tank units fielded a number of experimental Shermans such as this.

Their destruction came as they attempted to break out from the town, halted by the M5A1s of the 716th Tank Battalion. Japanese losses at Munoz were 10 Type 97s, one Type 95, and 247 troops. By March, the American forces had destroyed 203 Type 97 *Chi-Ha* tanks and 19 Type 95 *Ha-Go* tanks.

In many respects, the 2nd Armored Division had succeeded in delaying the American advance. But the IJA had nevertheless paid a terrible price. First, they had not succeeded in producing the amount of casualties that Yamashita had forecast. Second, the poor quality and maintenance of their tanks relegated most of them to semi-static defenses, which robbed the Type 97s and Type 95s of their greatest asset: mobility. Third, Yamashita's disdain for mechanized warfare had practically guaranteed that the IJA tanks would never see their full potential. Lastly, the IJA tanks themselves posed little threat to American armor. From the Luzon beaches to San Manuel and Munoz, even the pride of the IJA—the Type 97—was little match for the M4 Sherman.

Iwo Jima and Okinawa

As the Army tankers were reconquering the Philippine Islands, the Marines were preparing for their final showdowns on Iwo Jima and Okinawa. Much like Tarawa, the battle of Iwo Jima would go down in history as one of the most intense Marine Corps, operations of the Pacific War. Even the terrain of Iwo Jima was similar to Tarawa—a craggy volcanic island laced with a network of caves and extensive fortifications.

A Sherman belonging to the 5th Marine Tank Battalion falls victim to the soft volcanic soil on Iwo Jima, February 1945.

As the Allies closed in on the Japanese mainland, the IJA had begun realigning its doctrine, away from shoreline defense and more toward a battle of attrition within the confines of the inland terrain of the islands. They had done this on Peleliu and were concurrently doing likewise in the Philippines. Moreover, the IJA was adapting to the presence of American tanks. On Iwo Jima, for instance, the Japanese implemented the new Type 3 antitank mine, cased in ceramic so it could escape detection from conventional mine detectors.

The Iwo Jima defenders had several antitank guns, but the only armored asset on the island was the understrength 26th Tank Regiment, consisting of 22 newer Type 97 tanks. The regimental commander on Iwo Jima had hoped to employ his tanks as maneuver assets but, in keeping with the growing trends of the Japanese High Command, he was ordered to use them in static defense roles.

For the landings on Iwo Jima, the Marine Corps committed three of its tank battalions: the 3rd, 4th, and 5th. Together, these three battalions were the largest consolidated Marine

Comet, from Charlie Company, 4th Marine Tank Battalion, takes pause during the battle for Iwo Jima. Note "Widow Maker" on the barrel. It was not uncommon for tank crews to give separate names to their tank and their main gun.

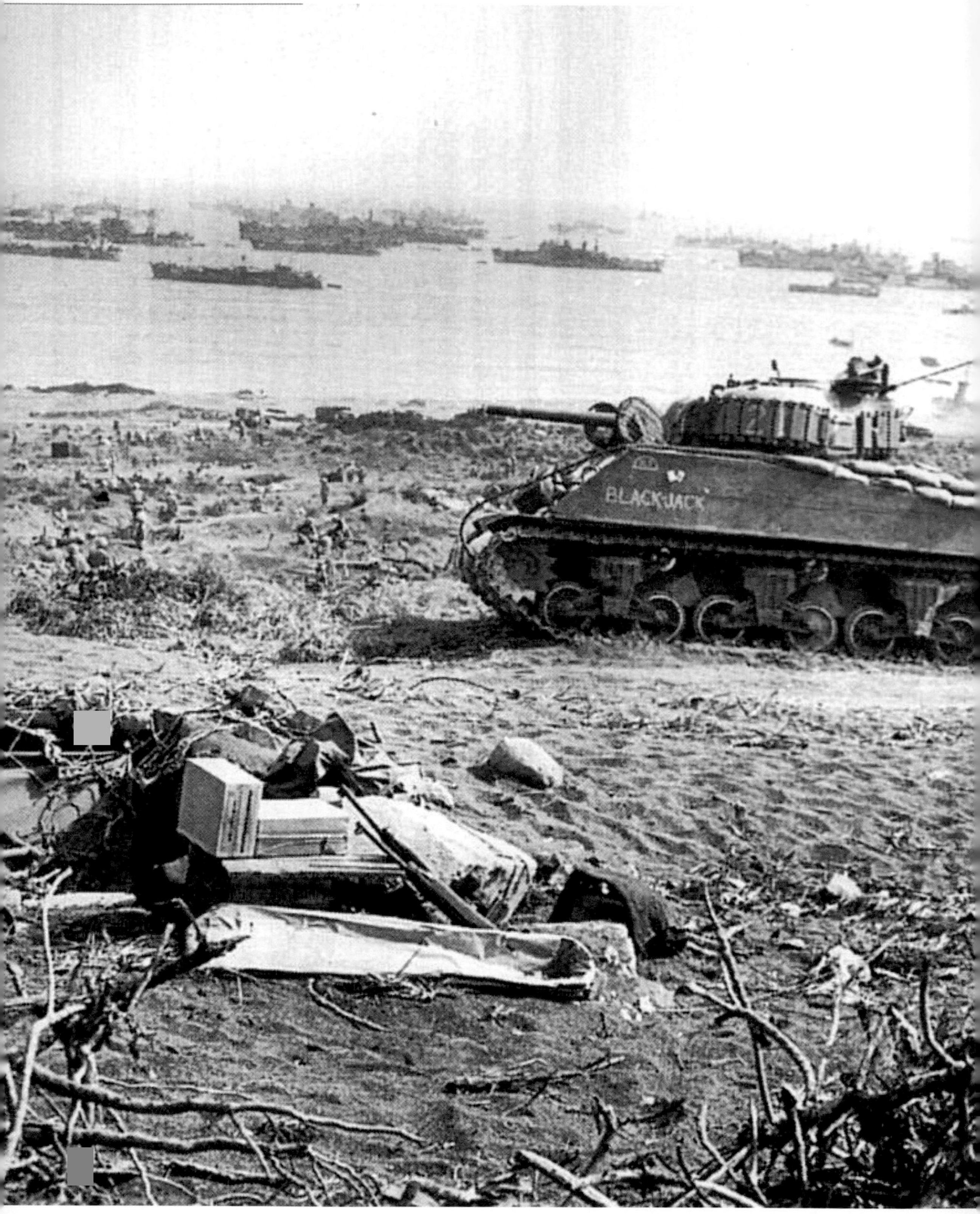
BLACKJACK

A pair of tanks from Baker Company, 4th Marine Tank Battalion at Blue Beach #2 on Iwo Jima, with the massive invasion fleet in the background.

An M4A2 Sherman from the 3rd Marine Tank Battalion leaves its landing craft and sallies forward onto the beaches of Iwo Jima.

tank force of the Pacific Theater. Wading ashore on February 19, 1945, the Marine Corps Shermans provided critical fire support to the infantry and were instrumental in overcoming the Japanese bunkers. By now, the bunker-busting tactics had been refined into a system known as the "corkscrew and blowtorch," wherein the tanks would suppress the bunker with main gun and machine-gun fire, while the infantry applied satchel charges, followed by a blaze from the nearest flamethrower tank. In fact, the Marines made such extensive use of the flamethrowing tanks that, on one day alone, the 5th Tank Battalion expended more than 5,000 gallons of fuel for their four "Zippo" tanks.

However, bunkers, enemy tanks, and antitank mines notwithstanding, it often seemed that the greatest hindrance to tank operations on Iwo Jima was the soft volcanic soil. Throughout the campaign, Marine Corps tanks often threw their tracks or otherwise got

During a lull in the fighting, Sherman crews from the 5th Marine Tank Battalion move into a bivouac area on Iwo Jima, February 1945.

In Profile:
1st Amphibian Tractor Battalion

The 1st Amphibian Tractor Battalion was activated February 16, 1942 at New River, North Carolina, as part of the 1st Marine Division. Equipped with the new LVT-series Alligator amtracs, the battalion was a pioneer in amphibious landing craft during the Pacific War. Following its stellar performance at Guadalcanal, Peleliu, and Okinawa, the battalion was deactivated in November 1945, but reactivated at Camp Pendleton the following year. The amtrac battalion further participated in the Korean War (Pusan Perimeter), Vietnam (Da Nang), and in Operation *Iraqi Freedom*. Eventually, renamed the "Combat Assault Battalion," the unit was finally deactivated in October 2018 and its assets parceled out to the rest of the 3rd Marine Division.

Marines from the 1st Amphibian Tractor Battalion assault the beaches on Guadalcanal, 1942.

stuck on the unstable terrain. To make matters worse, the soft pumice soil facilitated the IJA's use of antitank mines. Because of the soil type, even a smaller mine could disable a Sherman. Moreover, if the crew attempted to repair the vehicle on the battlefield, they were often cut down by small-arms fire. In fact, more tank crewmen were wounded from small-arms fire in this manner than by enemy tanks or antitank weapons.

For the battle proper, the 5th Tank Battalion spearheaded the initial assault on Mount Suribachi while the 4th Tank Battalion participated in the strike on Iwo Jima's airfields. On February 24, all three Marine tank battalions attempted to seize Airfield #2, but did not take the objective until three days later due to the high concentration of antitank mines and heavy antitank fire. In fact, the IJA's new tactics of using minefields and a network of underground fortifications along with heavy indirect fire support prompted the Marines to change their own tank-infantry tactics. According to the 4th Tank Battalion's after-action report:

> Due to the rugged terrain encountered on Iwo, orthodox infantry-tank tactics had to be abandoned. Tank tactics were improvised and, in many cases, basic principles of employment were disregarded. This was never done because of ignorance of fundamentals; it was done because the tactical situation warranted

A column from the 3rd Marine Tank Battalion moves forward during the assault on Airport 2 on Iwo Jima. February 24, 1945.

The crew of *Davy Jones*, a Sherman from the 5th Marine Tank Battalion, performs a pre-combat check of the vehicle. Note the wooden plank armor, a safeguard against Japanese magnetic mines.

certain calculated risks. Tank units were eager to support the infantry, and they did everything physically and mechanically possible to furnish that support. If it is certain that tank support of infantry and vice versa was less on Iwo than in previous operations, it is equally certain that the terrain encountered made this a foregone conclusion.

Marine tank losses were high. For instance, the 3rd Tank Battalion lost 15 of its 49 tanks. In the 4th Tank Battalion, nearly one in five men were casualties. Throughout the battle, both the 4th and 5th Tank Battalions had trouble keeping their vehicle numbers at half-strength, the biggest culprits of attrition being antitank mines.

Notwithstanding these losses, the Marines captured and secured Iwo Jima in what became one of the most iconic defeats for the Japanese in the Pacific Theater. According to the 9th Marine Regiment's after-action report, the attendant Marine tank battalions had been "the most effective supporting weapon in this action." The IJA seemed to agree. Even before Iwo Jima, the Japanese knew that they had to mitigate American tanks if they wished to prevail against U.S. forces in battle.

Fresh from their victory on Iwo Jima, U.S. forces assembled the largest Army–Marine amphibious force to date to assault the island of Okinawa, in April 1945. After the devastating defeat of the IJA's 2nd Armored Division in the Philippines, the Japanese High Command decided to reserve the best of its armored forces for the defense of the mainland. As on Iwo Jima, the Japanese had only one understrength tank regiment defending Okinawa. This paltry 27th Tank Regiment had only 13 Type 95s and 14 Type 97 *Shinhoto Chi-Ha* tanks. The Americans, on the other hand, committed the largest combined tank force of the Pacific Theater: eight Army tank battalions (including the 193rd Tank Battalion and the 713rd Flamethrower Tank Battalion), two Marine tank battalions (the battle-hardened 1st Tank

Coed, from Charlie Company in the 4th Marine Tank Battalion at the edge of Motoyama Airfield on Iwo Jima.

Battalion and the untested 6th Tank Battalion), two amphibious tank battalions, and two independent Marine tank companies. In total, this combined armored force contained more than 800 tanks.

As they had done elsewhere in the Pacific, American tanks performed exceptionally and facilitated the destruction of enemy forces. The 1st Tank Battalion highlighted the tight synchronicity of the tank-infantry team. According to the battalion's after-action report:

> At no time did tanks operate beyond the observation and cover of the infantry. Terrain and density as well as the type of enemy underground defenses precluded successful [tank] attack and none was attempted by this battalion. Such tactics at times attempted by the Tenth Army tank units [notably the 193rd Tank Battalion] met with disaster in each case … A highly effective, battle-proven Tank-Infantry SOP [standard operating procedure] had been used in training and numerous refinements in the technique of employment had been developed to a high degree prior to this operation.

Part and parcel to these tank-infantry tactics was a distinction between the enemy positions that were protected by underground fortifications, and those that were not. For the latter, the target was destroyed by artillery and tank main gun fire, followed by infantry seizing the ground surrounding the target. If an objective was supported by underground fortifications, however, it would be liquidated using a carefully planned system of tank-infantry teamwork. With the riflemen protecting their flanks, selected tanks would engage the enemy with

Nightmare II was a replacement tank sent to the 5th Tank Battalion during the ongoing fight for Iwo Jima. The battered tank is pictured here shortly before the end of fighting.

A close-up of a Sherman from Charlie Company, 4th Tank Battalion on Iwo Jima. The targeting clock painted on the rear was a reference for Marine infantrymen who used the attached infantry phone (note the canvas cover on the left, labeled "PHONE") to speak to the tank crew. It reminded the infantry soldiers to identify targets according to clock directions, e.g. 12 o'clock high.

A Sherman-based recovery vehicle in the foothills of Mount Suribachi on Iwo Jima.

Shermans from the 4th Tank Battalion during a hasty resupply on Iwo Jima.

1st Marine Tank Battalion in action on Okinawa, April 1945.

Shermans from the 1st Marine Tank Battalion hauling lumber on Okinawa. The timber was intended to fill Japanese antitank ditches.

Tanks from the 713th Tank Battalion take up positions on Okinawa in April 1945.

Marine tanks on patrol near Naha on Okinawa. For improvised appliqué armor, these tanks attached track blocks to the fronts and sides of the tanks.

A similarly retrofitted Sherman on Okinawa.

suppressing fire, while other tanks would simultaneously blast the enemy defenses, followed quickly thereafter by flamethrower tanks. The Marines repeated this process every 500 yards or so—clearing and securing enemy terrain along the way.

While the Marines were largely successful in their tank-infantry operations, some of their Army counterparts did not enjoy similar success. The 193rd Tank Battalion, for example, while supporting the U.S. Army's 27th Infantry Division, had a disastrous encounter with the IJA's 22nd Antitank Battalion on April 19, 1945. At 0830, a group of about 30 tanks and self-propelled guns, led by Able Company, 193rd Tank Battalion departed their assembly area via the Kakazu Gorge en route to enemy positions in the town proper. The American tanks shook out in groups of three and four, moving across the gorge in column formation. As the column descended into the gorge, however, three tanks were lost to enemy mines. Shortly thereafter, an IJA 47mm antitank gun opened fire from a covered position along a nearby ridge, destroying four tanks with 16 shots. Startled by the sudden onslaught of enemy fire, the tank column hurried south, looking for a trail into Kakazu proper. Along the way, Able Company lost another tank to enemy fire before ambling into the town shortly after 1000 hours. Upon encountering the enemy, Able Company's remaining tanks blazed through the village, engaging targets of opportunity in what became a three-hour firefight. Although the Army tankers accounted for several enemy dead, the Americans had needlessly lost 14 tanks in and around the village, victims of antitank mines and the dreaded 47mm antitank guns. Six were lost to suicide bombers, and some crewmen were needlessly killed by grenades thrown into open turret hatches.

By 1330, the beleaguered tanks were ordered to return to their lines. Of the 30 tanks that had departed for the Kakazu Gorge that morning, only eight returned that afternoon. The 22 tanks destroyed that day in Kakazu was the greatest loss suffered by American

A flamethrower tank from the 713th Tank Battalion, blazes an enemy position on Okinawa, May 17, 1945.

121

A crew from Able Company, 711th Tank Battalion, repairs a thrown track while under sniper fire on Okinawa. June 16, 1945.

A U.S. Army flamethrower tank blazes an enemy-occupied cave along the southern shores of Okinawa.

Perhaps the most ill-fated of the U.S. Army's tank units in the Pacific was the 193rd Tank Battalion. Like its sister battalions, the 192nd and 194th, the 193rd Tank Battalion was a National Guard unit called into federal service. When it deployed to the Pacific it was the only Army unit in the theater to employ the M3 Lee medium tank, a problematic machine that caused more issues than solutions. Although the 193rd eventually received Shermans, the battalion's performance during the battle of Okinawa was a disaster. By the end of the engagement, the battalion had been pared down to the point of combat ineffectiveness. The shattered battalion was then subsumed into the 983rd Field Artillery Battalion, marking its conversion into an indirect-fire unit.

armor in the Pacific Theater in a single day. Reviewing the engagement, it was clear that the tanks had been handicapped without their attendant infantry support. As seen elsewhere in the Pacific Theater—mostly notably in the Philippines and on Iwo Jima—tanks operated best in such an environment when operating as a tank-infantry team.

Tactical hiccups aside, Okinawa proved to be a resounding victory for the Army–Marine amphibious force. Following the Japanese defeat on Okinawa, General Lemuel C. Shepherd, commander of the 6th Marine Division, remarked that "if any one supporting arm can be singled out as having contributed more than any other during the progress of the campaign, the tank would certainly have to be selected."

By the end of the battle for Okinawa, the U.S. Army had become more adept in adding appliqué armor to its Shermans, as pictured here. On its side, the tank bears the words "392nd Avenger," a nod to its sister unit, the 392nd Tank Battalion, which fell at Bataan three years earlier.

| Afterword

Following the nuclear devastation of Hiroshima and Nagasaki, the Empire of Japan finally surrendered on September 2, 1945. With the downfall of the Imperial government, the Imperial Japanese Army formally ceased to exist. All the World War II-era Japanese tanks were scrapped as the Japanese armed forces officially reinvented themselves as the Japanese Self-Defense Forces.

As for the Americans, the conduct of their tanks in the Pacific had validated the use of armor in unconventional environments. The rapid territorial advances and conquests made by Japan between 1937 and 1942 had shown Western analysts the viability of tank warfare in the Pacific. The attendant challenge, though, was building an armored platform capable of standing toe to toe against the Japanese, and adapting that platform to the concepts of amphibious warfare.

In battles large and small, the American tank crews overcame considerable challenges against a battle-hardened enemy. In the face of aggressive antitank tactics and near-impenetrable bunkers, U.S. forces developed indomitable tank-infantry teams and fielded the infamous flame-throwing vehicles. In the tank-versus-tank battles the Sherman was almost always the victor. The Stuart, though not as successful as its heavier stablemate, nevertheless scored an impressive record throughout its service in the war.

Yet, for as cunning and audacious as the Japanese armored units could be, it seemed inevitable that they were destined to fail. Even the best Japanese tanks could not stand against American Shermans or tank destroyers. From the Type 89 to the Type 97, every IJA tank was under-armored, under-powered, and mechanically troublesome. The poor quality of the tanks themselves was compounded by the growing scarcity of fuel, spare parts, and maintenance personnel.

Furthermore, it seemed that IJA field commanders could not agree or remain consistent in applying their tactical doctrines. Indeed, throughout the war, Japanese tank tactics ranged from suicidal *banzai* charges to haphazard passive defenses. The American tactics varied as well: Marines tended to be more aggressive in using their tank battalions than the Army. Marines preferred to use tanks as the spearhead element, and insisted on tank-infantry synchronicity. The Army, on the other hand, often lacked the synergy of the tank-infantry team, tending to use their tanks as backup assets, and only when certain high-value targets had been identified. The Army did, however, excel in one area where their Marine Corps brethren did not: ironically, the Army's amphibious tank battalions were more adept at conducting shoreline attacks.

Whether under the U.S. Army or the U.S. Marine Corps, the American tank units in the Pacific Theater served with tenacity, dedication, and a spirit of innovation. From the near-decrepit state of America's prewar military, these tank crewmen rose to challenge the battle-hardened Japanese military, an enemy whose violence and brutality had made them the scourge of the Far East. America's victory in the Pacific, therefore, not only underscored the viability of tank warfare in the tropics, it also represented the triumph over the vicious imperialism that Japan had needlessly wrought upon its neighbors.

| Further Reading

Cameron, Robert S. *Mobility, Shock, and Firepower: The Emergence of the U.S. Army's Armor Branch, 1917–1945*. Washington DC: U.S. Government Printing Office, 2008.

Gilbert, Oscar E. *Tanks in Hell: A Marine Corps Tank Company on Tarawa*. Havertown: Casemate Publishers, 2015.

Gilbert, Oscar E., and E. Gilbert. *Marine Tank Battles in The Pacific*. Boston: Da Capo Press, 2007.

Giuliani, Raymond. *Sherman in the Pacific: 1943–1945*. Paris: Histoire et Collections, 2014.

Hofmann, George F., and Donn A. Starry. *Camp Colt to Desert Storm: The History of U.S. Armored Forces*. Lexington: University Press of Kentucky, 2013.

Salecker, Gene E. *Rolling Thunder Against the Rising Sun: The Combat History of U.S. Army Tank Battalions in the Pacific in World War II*. Mechanicsville: Stackpole Books, 2008.

Yeide, Harry. *The Infantry's Armor: The U.S. Army's Separate Tank Battalions in World War II*. Mechanicsville: Stackpole Books, 2010.

Zaloga, Steven J. *Armored Thunderbolt: The U.S. Army Sherman in World War II*. Mechanicsville: Stackpole Books, 2008.

_____. *Armour of the Pacific War*. Oxford: Osprey Publishing, 1983.

_____. *M4 Sherman vs Type 97 Chi-Ha: The Pacific 1945*. Oxford: Osprey Publishing, 2012.

_____. *Tank Battles of the Pacific War: 1941–1945*. Hong Kong: Concord Publishing, 1995.

_____. *U.S. Flamethrower Tanks of World War II*. London: Bloomsbury Publishing, 2013.

_____. *U.S. Marine Corps Tanks of World War II*. London: Bloomsbury Publishing, 2012.

Index

41, 43, 48, 53–55, 57–58, 61, 63, 65, 67–68, 84, 98, 100, 124
    M3 6, 8, 17–18, 20, 23–26, 30, 32, 34, 36, 37, 40, 43, 53, 55, 67
    M3A1 25, 39–41, 44, 48, 54–55, 57, 60–61, 65, 69–70, 73
    M5A1 26, 58, 60–61, 67, 72, 84, 98–99, 101, 104
    "Satan" flamethrower 67, 69–70, 73
Suzuki, Gen Teiichi 11

Takaki, 1Lt Yoshitaka 89, 92
Tarawa, battle of 6, 8, 40, 44, 46–51, 53, 57, 72, 79–80, 84, 104
    Betio islet 6, 44, 46, 50, 55
Tinian, battle of 72–73, 77–79, 84
Tripartite Pact 10

United States Armed Forces Far East 32–34
    Asiatic Fleet 32
    Far East Air Force 32
    1st Provisional Tank Group 32, 34
U.S. Army 6, 7, 9, 19–21, 24–25, 27, 30, 41, 43, 53, 57, 59, 65, 71, 80, 86–88, 91, 98, 121–124
    Sixth Army 8
    Tenth Army 114
    National Guard 32–33, 123
    By Corps
      I Corps 87, 96
      XIV Corps 87
    By Division
      1st Cavalry Division 95
      7th Infantry Division 57, 61
        708th Tractor/Tank Battalion (Provisional) 61, 63, 65, 69
      25th Infantry Division 99–100
      27th Infantry Division 72, 121
      37th Infantry Division 42
      43rd Infantry Division 88, 91, 96
      77th Infantry Division 73
      81st Infantry Division 80
      96th Infantry Division 86
    By Tank Battalion
      13th Armored Group 87–88
      18th Armored Group 88

      44th 84, 87–88, 101
      192nd 6, 32–34, 123
      193rd 7, 53, 55, 57, 113–114, 121, 123
      194th 6, 32–34, 123
      392nd 123
      706th 7, 73, 75, 93
      713th Flamethrower 7, 119, 121
      716th 7, 87–89, 92–93, 95–96, 98–99, 101, 104
      745th 43
      754th 8, 43, 47, 87–88, 99
      762nd 67–68, 71
      766th 63, 71
      767th 7, 43, 57, 59–61
      775th 43, 88, 93, 98, 102
      603rd Separate Tank Company 41
U.S. Marine Corps 6, 9, 19, 21–22, 24, 30, 44, 50–51, 124
    1st Division 40, 80–82, 110
    2nd Division 40, 44, 46, 65, 72
    3rd Division 73, 110
    4th Division 59, 65, 69, 72
    6th Division 123
    1st Provisional Marine Brigade 73
    By Tank Battalion
      I Marine Amphibious Corps
      3rd Amphibious Tractor
      4th Amphibious Tractor
      1st 6–7, 24–25, 36, 81–83, 113–114, 117
      2nd 6, 40, 50, 71, 72, 77–78
      3rd 7, 41, 65, 108, 111
      4th 7, 57–60, 66–67, 69, 71–72, 79, 105, 107, 113
      5th 104, 109, 112
U.S. Navy 10, 23, 83
    Pacific Fleet 10

Vickers Medium C tank 11

Wada, WO Kojura 95
Wake Island 36
War Department (U.S.) 21, 24, 36
White Motor Company 31

Yamashita, Gen Tomiyuki 85–87, 104